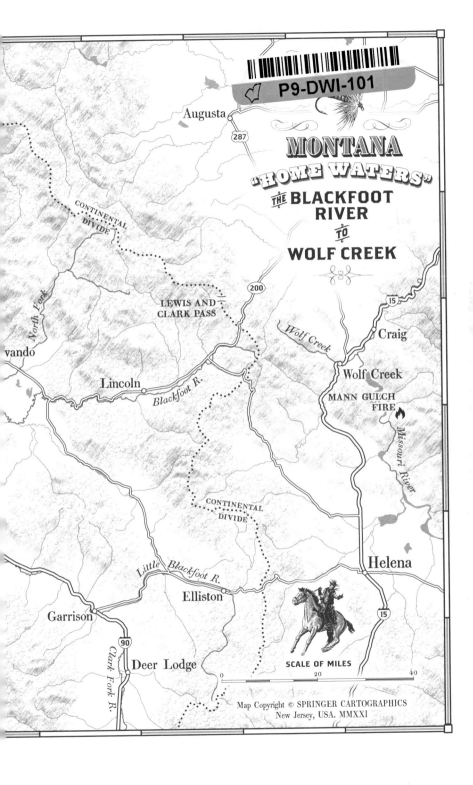

P9-DWI-101

MONTANA
"HOME WATERS"
THE BLACKFOOT RIVER
TO
WOLF CREEK

Augusta

287

CONTINENTAL DIVIDE

North Fork

LEWIS AND CLARK PASS

200

Wolf Creek

15

Craig

Wolf Creek

MANN GULCH FIRE

vando

Lincoln

Blackfoot R.

Missouri River

CONTINENTAL DIVIDE

Little Blackfoot R.

Elliston

Helena

Garrison

15

90

Clark Fork R.

Deer Lodge

SCALE OF MILES

0   20   40

Map Copyright © SPRINGER CARTOGRAPHICS
New Jersey, USA. MMXXI

HOME WATERS

JOHN N. MACLEAN

HOME WATERS

A Chronicle of Family and a River

Wood Engravings
by Wesley W. Bates

CUSTOM
HOUSE

HarperCollins books may be purchased for educational, business, or sales promotional use. For information, please email the Special Markets Department at SPsales@harpercollins.com.

FIRST EDITION

Designed by Lucy Albanese
Wood engravings by Wesley W. Bates
Endpaper map by Nick Springer/Springer Cartographics LLC

Library of Congress Cataloging-in-Publication Data

Names: Maclean, John N., author. | Bates, Wesley W., illustrator.

Title: Home waters : a chronicle of family and a river / John N. Maclean ; wood engravings by Wesley W. Bates.

Description: First edition. | New York, NY : Custom House, [2021] | Includes index.

Identifiers: LCCN 2020051044 | ISBN 9780062944597 (hardcover) | ISBN 9780062944603 (trade paperback) | ISBN 9780062944610 (ebook)

Subjects: LCSH: Maclean, John N. | Maclean, John N.—Family. | Journalists—United States—Biography. | Fishers—United States—Biography. | Fly fishing—Montana—Blackfoot River. | Blackfoot River (Mont.)—Biography. | Blackfoot River (Mont.)—Description and travel. | Montana—Biography.

Classification: LCC F737.B62 M33 2021 | DDC 978.6/615—dc23

LC record available at https://lccn.loc.gov/2020051044

ISBN 978-0-06-294459-7

21 22 23 24 25 LSC 10 9 8 7 6 5 4 3 2 1

To Dan, JohnFitz, Jacob, Noah, Jodi
and their families

CONTENTS

HOME WATERS

ON THE BIG BLACKFOOT

THE TROUT ROSE in a smooth arc, took my tumbling salmon fly, and completed its curve in an undulating, revelatory sequence. A greenish speckled back and a flash of scarlet on silver along its side marked it as a rainbow. One slow beat, set the hook . . . in those first seconds I felt a connection to a fish of great size and power.

This could be the one.

I've fished the Blackfoot River in northwestern Montana from the time I was big enough to tag along with my father and the other men of my family, yearning for the day when I, like them, would catch an enormous rainbow trout, the river's signature fish. Over the decades the heft of the rainbow necessary to reach that landmark had advanced with my age and proficiency, and I had never quite achieved it.

It was clear this trout would set the terms of the fight: he wasn't a fish to be horsed. There were no logjams or iceberg rocks around, and he had deep waters to work with—the Muchmore Hole on the Blackfoot River in northwestern Montana, made famous by my father, Norman Maclean, in his novella, *A River Runs through It*. Old-timers will tell you there are several "Muchmore Holes" on the river, the very name speaking of bounty. (There are even more "Muchless Holes.") This one, however, is named for the Muchmore family, who homesteaded here in 1895. It also perfectly resembles a description in the book, that of an epic fight my father had with a big rainbow, the fish rising in swirling foam from an apparently bottomless hole below a rock reef.

The features all match: The Muchmore Hole begins with a long and relatively shallow rapid. The water pours over a reef of rock extending unevenly for the width of the river. Past the reef, the river turns back on itself in a giant whirlpool for half its width, swirling foam covering much of the whirlpool's surface. The other half of the hole, where I was fishing on that June afternoon, is a long, powerful rapid. When I was young, the Muchmore Hole was a great mystery, a place where the fish practically jumped into your basket—except there was no way for me to get there. When I asked my dad why we didn't fish there, he told me he no longer knew who owned the ranch bordering that stretch of the river and couldn't get access. But he also held many memories close, in a kind of time vault, to be reshaped and burnished without the nuisance of updates.

Long years after my childhood, the ranch earned a new owner, a Chicago businessman named Jay Proops. I'd struck up a friendship with him back in the Midwest where I worked as a newsman for the *Chicago Tribune*. When we first met, Jay and his wife, Kay, had just made a trip west to explore the actual scenes in my dad's book, which they loved. They now dreamed of owning a ranch on the Blackfoot River. They'd found one, but the price was too dear. I encouraged them, though, and their business prospered, and eventually their dream came true, for me as well as for them. They bought the ranch, including riverfront on the Muchmore Hole, and they often invited me over to fish at their place, not far from our family cabin at Seeley Lake. When I finally saw the storied water, what had been for me a long-sought mirage, always beyond reach, suddenly became real.

The Muchmore Hole didn't look promising on that bright and windy day when Jay and I walked down the bank to fish it. The sun played on the rushing water and gave it a hard metallic sheen. The fish most likely were down in the depths to avoid eyestrain. I set up my rod, waded out a few steps toward the long rapid on the near side of the hole, and shook out some line. Then I flipped a cast toward the top of the rapid, in a pocket where it broke over the reef. There I hooked the biggest rainbow I've ever seen on the Blackfoot. I carefully measured and weighed the fish in my mind: over twenty-four inches, more than six pounds.

Jay watched as the trout broached. "It's like a salmon!" he shouted. He put down his rod and reached for his long-handled net.

This rainbow was big and strong, and he fought his battle in heavy water where he used the strength of the river to magnify his own. The line went taut to the reel—an old-style Ross Gunnison G2—which spun as the fish plunged and thrashed down the long rapid. The rod was a new one—a made-in-Montana R.L. Winston nine-foot, five-weight Boron III X—and I'd already lost fish adjusting to the famed soft action tip. The outfit was well suited to normal conditions, but this rainbow was exceptional from the moment of the rolling take. I followed along and kept the rod tip up and the pressure on, not hard but firm. When I was young, I lost a lot of big fish by not trusting the tackle—or myself—and holding on too hard, giving the fish a firm brace to shake off the hook. I could not lose this trout that way, I told myself. I'd spent too many decades pursuing this moment: the past haunted the present. In such a contest, seconds and minutes expand into timeless, defining moments.

A long battle is exhilarating for a fisherman but can be exhausting or even fatal for a fish, and a responsible sportsman tries to bring it to hand and release it without delay. The fish, however, gets a say in this. Jay waded out with the net and prepared for the capture, except the rainbow glimpsed the net and didn't like what he saw. He broached and twisted as the current inched him downriver toward the net. Jay swooped up the net, but the trout was too big for it and sprawled half in, half out. He escaped back into the water and we had to start the process all over. Jay tried again with the net and failed once more. I began yelling at my friend because I couldn't understand why he didn't just net the fish and finish the thing. In a rush of anxiety, I tightened up on the line, the same overreaction that had cost me battles when I was a kid. I was about to lose the fish of a lifetime.

CHAPTER ONE

TWO WORLDS, ONE CABIN

MANY GO THROUGH life without glimpsing Heaven and
Hell, but fishing with my father gave me an early appreci-
ation of both places. Hell was when I lost a big fish in front
of him. "What did I bring you here for? How could you
have muffed him? You muffed him!" When I hooked a big
fish, however, he became so enthusiastic that on occasion he
joined the fight.

When I was barely in my teens, my dad and I went fishing on the Swan River, a favorite alternative to the Blackfoot. The Swan is smaller water, but it can surprise you. On
this trip, I tied into a rainbow of about a pound and a half,
a real monster for the Swan. The trout put up an enormous
battle and my father, to make sure I didn't mess up my big
chance, waded into the water below the fish and began to

shoo him up to me, splashing the water and damn near touching the fish. The last thing you want is for a fighting fish to touch or be touched by something solid, to give it the leverage required to slip the fly. Despite the help I landed the fish. When the rainbow at last flopped onto the bank, my father's face filled with a kind of rapture, and he knelt down, picked up the trout, and held it up, beaming the way God must smile on those entering Heaven.

My father taught me to love fishing, but he did not teach me how to fish. If you wonder at that, consider this story by a dear friend of his, a distinguished literary critic from the University of Chicago, Wayne Booth. When Wayne and his wife, Phyllis, once visited Seeley Lake, my father took them to the lakeshore for a lesson in how to fish with a fly rod.

"We spent the whole day, casting and casting, with his precise instructions about just which position of the clock our elbows and shoulders and heads should be in. I naturally kept wondering, as my shoulders began to ache, why, with all this developing skill, we were catching no fish. Only at the end of the day, as we were returning to the cabin, did he confess that on that kind of day, with that kind of light, that kind of water, and that kind of insect in the air, there had not been a chance in the world of our catching anything. We could easily have caught dozens of fish if we'd been willing to do it wrong, to fish in some other way—with a worm, say. But the point was not to catch any old fish in any old way, but to catch the right fish in the right way."

My formal apprenticeship as a fisherman began one day when my father and I, along with George Croonenberghs, an old family friend and fishing partner, hiked to Morrell Creek, a small, hard-to-fish stretch of water in a mountain valley near the cabin. I must have been close to teenage, because getting in and out of that steep, brush-and-timber-choked valley could be brutal, impassable for children. Morrell Creek rises from snow and ice on rugged mountaintops at the southern end of the Swan Range and cascades down a series of waterfalls, then enters a lake and winds its way to the Clearwater River. From there, it joins up with the Blackfoot. The water is so cold we called it Ice Cream Creek, and so pure we used to get our drinking water from it where it flowed under a bridge after a long run down from the mountains. Spruce trees and brush line the banks and drape over the water, shielding it from the sun and keeping it cold while making it difficult to cast a fly. Logjams dot the creek, perfect hiding places for the native westslope cutthroat trout that spawn there.

Westslope cutthroat have a soft, fawn-like beauty. Crimson slashes mark the undersides of the jaw and there's a light brushstroke of reddish-brown along the white underbelly. Dark spots speckle their greenish-brown backs, blending perfectly with the creek bottom if you or another predator look down at them from above. The cutthroat in Morrell Creek were deeply colored, each one a piece of fine art. On this trip I repeatedly snagged my fly in spruce trees and brush, causing much lost fishing time. George, who at six feet four inches towered over us, did most of the extricating, but my many snags caused frustration all around. When it had happened once too often, my father turned to me and said, not unkindly, "From here on, you're with him. Do what he tells you and shows you to do." This marked the start of my lifelong bond with a man who progressively became my hero, tutor, companion, and oldest friend.

George Croonenberghs was born into a family of giants, three brothers all well over six feet tall. George didn't start out at six feet four inches, of course. In fact, he was the little kid, the youngest as he grew up with his brothers Al and Boyd, who were respectively six feet seven inches and six feet three inches tall.

The Croonenberghs lived next door to the Macleans for a time in Missoula, and the two families built cabins next to each other at Seeley Lake. Being the youngest—born thirteen years after my father—George got left behind when the older boys went off to fish. My grandfather and namesake, the Rev. John Norman Maclean, took note of George's abandoned state and invited him over to the cabin, where he taught him to tie flies. The two of them would sit on the cabin's screened porch and work at a tying vise until it got too windy and then they'd move inside, where they had to negotiate space with Mrs. Maclean. "I used to go to see the Reverend," said George, "but you had to be careful. You had to apply to Mrs. Maclean to see if it was okay. Sometimes she'd say, 'No, the Reverend is taking his nap,' or she'd say, 'No, he's studying, you'll have to come back another time.'"

The Reverend Maclean and George tied flies out of any odd material they could find: scraps of yarn, bits of cotton, cork bottle stoppers, whatever was lying around. Over time their skills improved, the materials became uniform, the flies worked, and naturally the other boys took advantage of George's new skill, poaching flies off him for free. George never seemed to mind, and even late in life generously made flies for friends, presenting them in miniature cardboard boxes he'd also made himself. The Reverend took George fishing with him on the Blackfoot when he was too young to fish big water but not to carry the older man's creel. George would stand on the bank with the basket straps draped over his then-small frame and watch his mentor adoringly.

As he grew older, George began to display rare gifts as

a fisherman. He eventually became friends with my uncle Paul, like him the youngest brother. Paul would hide in the bushes and throw rocks into holes where George was fishing, trying to fool him into thinking the splashes were fish and not incidentally spoiling George's chances for a better catch than Paul's.

By the time I came along, George had become master of the Blackfoot River, the one who could cast the farthest, bring home the heaviest basket of fish, and create stout flies that were nearly infallible. George's yellow quill fly was his most popular pattern, a fly for all seasons that imitates a wide variety of insect life. It was the first fly we pulled out of our fly boxes. The yellow quill has caught fish from Montana to Alaska to the more tender rivers of the East, and abroad. George dyed the quills for the fly bodies himself, not trusting pre-dyed versions from a catalog.

"If you want to know a secret, I'll tell you one," George would say. "When I'm sitting beside a stream, trying to see what's driving the fish up, I try to get the flies between me and the sun. Not so much to see their color. That's important, but more important than color is radiance. How do they light up? Radiance is what makes the difference."

George put his flies up for sale in saloons and shops in Missoula, but making a name for himself in a crowded field proved difficult. He solved the problem one day when he caught a magnificent basketful of fish on a secret stretch of the Blackfoot. He displayed the catch at Bob Ward's sporting goods store, in a glass-covered case on a bed of ice, with a note: "Caught on the Croonenberghs Grasshopper on the Blackfoot River at Clearwater bridge." Of course, his secret spot was nowhere near there. For weeks afterward the Croonenberghs Grasshopper, a big cork thing that works only on occasion, was a sellout, and fishermen lined up basket to basket at the Clearwater bridge, which even back then was fished out.

George started our lessons on small water, where he taught me about plucking flies from spruce trees as well as about fishing. Fishing wasn't all about flies and casting, he said. You have to learn to think like a fish. For example, if you wanted food and shelter in a stream, where would you station yourself? The answer is, at different places at different times. A resting fish will go deep and dark, but a feeding fish will move to spots where there's an abundance of food: perhaps into fast water that's carrying half-drowned grasshoppers, or nosing the bottom to stir up cased caddis larvae, or just under a quiet surface awaiting a passing mayfly. George would sometimes deliberately walk back and forth through a hole, testing the bottom with his feet to get the fish's perspective.

When at last I grew big enough to join the men on the

Blackfoot River, I marked George's and my father's very different but complementary styles of fishing. Norman Maclean was a careful and patient fisher of trout. He would approach a hole as he would a book, by pausing first to assess the river—checking the table of contents, as it were. He worked a hole in a methodical manner so as not to spoil water before he could fish it. Fish face upstream, so he mostly started from the bottom and moved up, one casting distance at a time. He always started with a plan, even if it wasn't a perfect one. That's also precisely the way he spotted top students at the university: they were the ones who began with a theory, even if it didn't work out and later had to be discarded. His casts were precise but not particularly long. The only times I saw him make sloppy casts were when the wind took his line. He'd utter a wicked remark, settle himself down, and get his fly back out where the fish were.

He took fishing personally. If a promising hole failed to yield a rise, his shoulders would droop and he'd assume a beaten, downcast look. "How could such a beautiful piece of water be so refusing?" he'd say. Like the rest of us, he most often started with George's yellow quill, but he willingly tried every sort of fly, from dry flies to spinners and all stops in between. He liked to collect unusual flies like the now-famous cork Bunyan Bug, and his fly box was a riot of different colors and shapes. He lost flies, like everybody else, but I don't believe he ever threw one away. As a young man, he returned from Dartmouth with a spinning rod and daredevils, tackle seldom seen in Montana, and was wildly successful with the rig until everyone started doing it, and he went back to a fly rod.

Once he had a fish on, Norman almost never lost it. The throb of the fish running through the light wand joined for him the worlds of nature and the spirit, the seen with the unseen, just as they had been for his father before him. Always, Norman fished waters deeper than the river in front of him. After he finally slid a fish onto the bank, rushing only at the end when its head could be held out of water, he would muse out loud for a while, especially if it were a big fish. He liked an audience—even if only one teenage son—though it was clear he addressed a broader public even then. Standing on the bank with the fish in his hand like a teacher holding out a text, he would recount the details of the battle. Inevitably he turned his words to what his brother would have thought if he'd seen the show. Paul told him, he often said in his musing, that there was nobody as good as Norman at landing a fish, though Paul criticized him for lacking the aggressiveness he himself displayed in going after big fish in difficult water. Though he died before I was born, Paul became a presence with us on the river, a broad-shouldered figure with a slouch Stetson hat who would stop for a moment to admire my dad for his artfulness in playing a fish, but who then quickly moved on, happy in the knowledge that his creel was heavier and fuller than his brother's, and always would be.

Norman and George Croonenberghs took different water when they fished together, my father making the most of the holes that didn't require hero casts. They both fished quickly, but when they hopscotched past each other to move up to the next hole they would trade information on what fly was working, which insects they'd seen, and how many fish had been caught. Most vital was the question "Anything big?" They referred to size, of course, but also "significance," for even a moderately sized rainbow qualified for a respectful comment if it had put on a fine aerial display, as they often do. I studiously took note. For me, landing a rainbow trout of rare size and significance on the Blackfoot River became the way to gain entry into the pantheon of notable family fishers. Ambition comes easy when you're young; it's working it out later that gets hard. And I knew there was only one best, always the unseen Paul.

Unlike my father, George did not engage in preliminaries when he started to fish a hole. He aimed his first cast at the prime spot where he thought the largest fish would be, no working up to the big moment in lesser water. He made other casts after that one, of course, but his rule was that the initial cast into a hole was the vital one—fish don't get big by giving anglers second chances. When he lost a fish, which happens to the best of fishermen, he did not bemoan the loss but immediately cast into fresh water, moving on. He would stand hip deep in the Blackfoot River and cover water up, across, and down from him with powerful but seemingly effortless casts, on a scale none could match. When the three of us fished together, George was happy to spend most of the day together, trading observations with my dad or instructing me about making that perfect first cast into a likely hole.

As the sun dipped and the evening rise began, though, George often left us behind and disappeared into the gathering dusk. Off on his own, he could move swiftly over the slippery rocks, throw line clear across the river, and make precisely targeted casts into waters he knew by heart. Toward dark he'd come back to us, as my father and I sat huddled on the riverbank, small, wet, chilled, and tired. He had the grace of an ambling bear. Silhouetted against the last of the light, his big frame swung over rather than scrambled across the rocks. He stood poised on a big rock until he had figured out a series of steps, and then he'd drop gracefully from one to another with unexpected twists and turns. He arrived before us as a giant shadow, his hair thick and dark, his face bright with the joy of being master of the river. When he held out his fish basket, a forked tail stuck out one side with the snout of a giant rainbow trout out the other.

THE PHYSICAL LINK between Montana, where my parents were raised, and the Midwest, where they moved in adulthood, was the family cabin, a simple log affair built by my father's family in the 1920s at Seeley Lake, fifty-five road miles northeast of Missoula on the edge of what is now the million-plus-acre Bob Marshall Wilderness. The Maclean cabin has always been a lucky place. At the time my grandfather, the Reverend Maclean, obtained a Forest Service permit to build it, in 1921, the agency actively encouraged private recreational buildings on National Forest land, a policy that was abandoned with prejudice as recreational use of the public forests boomed in the decades after World War II. The cabin has survived a century of upheaval in federal land-use policy. It's near the public Seeley Lake campground, which became so popular that it regularly filled to overflowing. Two cabins stood between us and the campground, and the Forest Service ordered first one and then the other removed to create a buffer between campers and inholders, as we are called. Our cabin was next. Fortunately, the buffer worked, and the Maclean cabin is still there. It's been in family hands now for five generations and counting.

The Reverend Maclean obtained the first lease for the ground on August 8, 1921, covering the final quarter of the year for a fee of $3.34. Cutting logs for construction required an additional fee of $6.00, which was paid on January 6 of the following year. By then, other leaseholders had felled lodgepole pine trees around their sites at such an alarming rate that the Forest Service sent all leaseholders a notice forbidding further cutting of trees on or near their lots. Cheap, locally sourced wood was a godsend for the leaseholders, who were Montanans of ordinary means. As a substitute, the agency reserved a stand of lodgepole pine trees for cutting in a less scenic area. A sawmill then at the north end of the lake milled timber for floors, roofs, and other uses.

The Reverend Maclean took great care in picking a site for his cabin. He chose a spot far enough from the lakefront to avoid creating an eyesore for lake users, but close enough to have a panoramic view of the lake and the mountains beyond, the southern edge of the Swan Range. He and the Forest Service agreed to sacrifice the fewest possible giant western larch trees, part of an old-growth forest of hundreds of acres on that side of Seeley Lake. Larch drop their lower branches as they grow, which helps make them fire resistant, but are bushy near the top, which provides cover that functions as natural air-conditioning. One gigantic specimen located about a mile from the cabin is estimated to be a thousand years old and is rated the largest of its kind in North America. The Reverend had to fell one big larch to make room for the cabin, but he did not waste it. The tree was cut into blocks that were used as the cabin's foundation. (Over time, with the grain exposed to the elements, the blocks absorbed water, rotted, and had to be replaced by cinder blocks.)

Friends mocked the Reverend's architectural design, a modestly sloped pyramidal roof over the main room and nearly flat shed extensions over a porch to the east and a kitchen and bedroom to the west. The design—it looks like a tent with nearly horizontal flaps on either side—allows more interior space than the simple A-shaped roof favored by others, who warned his roof would succumb to the heavy snows of the Seeley Lake valley: it has leaked but not collapsed. The construction of the cabin took several years, beginning with a floor that served as a tent platform while the rest of the cabin arose around it. The Reverend Maclean had learned carpentry from his father, whose family had emigrated from Scotland in 1821 to farm in Nova Scotia, Canada. He had inherited a chest full of early-nineteenth-century tools—planes, drawknives, saws, augers—that were heavy, simple, and fit your hand. Their plain, graceful lines could pass for modern art, and we used them for decades until the chest was stolen in a winter break-in.

The walls went up slowly. The Reverend's sons, Norman and Paul, helped when they could, but they were tied up with summer jobs the year the roof was raised. The Reverend and Mrs. Maclean did that job alone. Decades later, when my father and I oiled the cabin logs, he would take a break now and then and gaze at the roof, trying to figure out how his parents had managed to erect it by themselves. The Reverend almost surely had made a travois or similar contraption with a block and tackle, and, working with his wife, pulled the framing timbers and stringers into place. Once those supports were up, a single worker could nail on the roof planking. There was an outhouse, of course, and they added a garage, a root cellar, and an icehouse, the latter essential in the days before electricity. A local handyman would take a horse-drawn sledge out onto Seeley Lake in the winter, cut blocks of ice, and store them in six feet of sawdust in the icehouse, where icy bits could be recovered as late as September.

The Reverend Maclean conducted marriages, baptisms, and other church activities at the cabin. A fading photograph shows a baptismal party for a prominent Missoula family, the Tooles, who pose outside the cabin with the Reverend, all parties wearing jackets and ties. One of the pictured youngsters, K. Ross Toole, became a much-beloved professor of history at the University of Montana and authored *Montana: An Uncommon Land,* which remains a standard history of the state. The Reverend Maclean's spirit is everywhere in that cabin, from the overall design to the saddle notches where the logs of the cabin walls join, one across the other. The notches, which he fashioned with a handsaw and hatchet, allow the logs to fit snugly together at the joints. Small gaps inevitably remain along the length of the logs, and those he caulked with oakum—loosely twisted jute or hemp fiber soaked in oil or tar. When I am rubbing the logs with linseed oil and turpentine, which the cabin needs every few years, the Reverend becomes almost a living presence.

FISHERMEN KNOW THE wonder of being attached to a living but unseen power that lies below the surface. The connection between my family, the Blackfoot River, and Montana has been like that, a tie rooted in memory and rekindled each year. As far back as I can remember, my family led two lives, one at our remote log cabin in Montana, a land of big skies, shining mountains, endless winters, and giant rainbow trout, and the other at a world-class institution of higher learning, the University of Chicago, in the flatlands of the Midwest. Our divided life followed seasonal rhythms, heading west for the long summer break of the academic year and wintering over in the Midwest. Keeping these vastly different worlds in contact and moving between them was no easy task, physically or mentally.

We didn't rush to leave Chicago for the annual cross-country trek because Montana even in June could be cold, wet, and miserable. One rain squall after another scudded down on a biting wind from Canada. The sun was an unfulfilled promise that peeked out in the rare breaks between fast-moving clouds. Montanans sometimes describe their climate as nine months of winter and three months of guests. It would be late June, then, before we were ready for our other life at Seeley Lake.

One spring, as the time to depart drew near, my father led me out onto the Midway, the elegant mile-long park on the southern edge of the University of Chicago, where he was a professor in the English department. "Come with me, I want you to see this," he said. He faced the university's Gothic-style buildings, which stretch in an unbroken line of gray Indiana limestone for blocks and blocks, resembling a medieval city. He put his thumb to his nose, wiggled his fingers, and gave the academic life the bird. A campus dormitory would be named Maclean House in his honor, but that time was far off.

My father needed both worlds, a high-powered intellectual life and the life of woods and rivers. If he had settled in Montana, working for the Forest Service or teaching high school, he might not have felt the strain of being apart from something he loved as deeply as he did Montana. This creative tension resolved itself in his seventh decade in a "love poem to my family," as he described *A River Runs through It*. Moreover, the family tragedy that inspires the novella, his brother Paul's murder, might not have happened were it not for this dislocation. In his bristly, difficult way, my father loved the University of Chicago. He knew it as a rough, tough academic community that was "hard on students" and gave no intellectual quarter. He liked that. He also found joy in students, at least the ones who could rebound from harsh treatment and produce quality work. He said they kept him young, and the good ones prevented him from going stale in courses repeated year after year. Especially rewarding were those who came back years later, inspired to say he'd changed their lives. He'd ask them what it was he'd said or done that had stuck with them. It was always a simple remark or quote, among them Wordsworth's "Act! Act in the living present!" He and my mother made lifelong contributions to the university and formed deep, abiding friendships there.

By late June of nearly every year, though, the balance had to be restored, and we left Chicago behind and hit the road, heading west. The four of us—my parents; my sister, Jean; and me—squeezed into a car as encumbered with baggage as a pack mule loaded for the backcountry. One of our secondhand black sedans was so plain my father said with a sigh that it would have made a proper preacher's car, one his father might have owned. As we started out full of the pioneer spirit, the black-dirt fields of northern Illinois sprouted new corn, fast on its way to being "knee high by the Fourth of July." The first dramatic event of the trip came as we crossed the Mississippi River on a venerable bridge that trembled alarmingly under the car, year after year.

Roads often traveled, though, acquire their own memorable landmarks. My dad joked that we'd followed the same route so often that he could let go of the wheel and the car would find its own way. True West for us began in Chamberlain, South Dakota, at the Missouri River crossing. As you come down the hills to the river, you leave behind the lush farmland of the Middle West and see across the river the rolling brown hills of the Great Plains stretching to the horizon. Only 150 miles ahead lie the Badlands and another landmark, Wall Drug, famous for the roadside model of an eighty-foot Brontosaurus reminding passersby that this desiccated landscape was once tropical and teemed with dinosaurs.

Not far beyond Wall Drug lie the Black Hills. When approached from the plains, it's easy to understand why the Sioux and other tribes regard them as sacred. After hundreds of miles of a flat dry landscape, they jut up on the horizon as an oasis—a winter haven and a year-round preserve of fish and game. They are a small, isolated mountain range, however, and beyond them in Wyoming lies another high-plains expanse. On June 26, 1950, we drove the forbidding hundred-mile stretch between Gillette and Sheridan listening to the radio and learned the Korean War had started the day before. The announcement seemed utterly out of place. "We're at war; it should feel different," said my mother as she looked out the window where nothing moved but heat waves.

We always pulled over at the sign for the Montana border, where we smiled and took pictures. Jean might try a cartwheel. It can take two full days to cross Montana by car—there's a reason they call it high, wide, and handsome. We most always stopped to spend a week at my mother's hometown of Wolf Creek to rest, fish, and renew family ties. My mother's brother, Ken Burns, and his wife, Dottie, had stayed on in Wolf Creek running a chicken ranch—this was Montana, where we called it a ranch, not a farm—while the rest of the Burns family scattered.

The final leg of the trip, over the Continental Divide to

Seeley Lake, was tortuous, largely on dirt roads heavily traf-
ficked by logging trucks. The most direct route from Wolf
Creek is over Rogers Pass, the headwaters of the Blackfoot
River, and then along Highway 200 through the Blackfoot
Valley, which roughly follows the route taken by Meriwether Lewis on the return journey of the Lewis and Clark
Expedition in July 1806. After passing through the town of
Lincoln, we entered the Blackfoot Canyon and caught the
first glimpses of the Blackfoot River, which meanders softly
along this stretch before the more characteristic heavy wa-
ter farther along.

At Clearwater Junction, near the confluence of the
Clearwater and Blackfoot rivers, we turned north on the
last leg of the cross-country odyssey. The Clearwater River
drains a chain of lakes including Seeley Lake in a long, narrow valley that was filled with a glacier in the last ice age.
Just south of Clearwater Junction, at the extreme extension
of the glacier, the ice shoved huge piles of till up against the
Garnet Range, which held them in check. After the glaciers began to melt about fifteen thousand years ago, what
became the Blackfoot River cut its way along the base of
the Garnet Range, slicing through the till near Clearwater
Junction and giving the river a special character. Because
the mountains form an impermeable barrier, much of the
river has retained its general shape for millennia. It's com-

forting to a fisherman to know that the great holes will be intact one year to another, one generation to the next.

As we drove north up the Clearwater drainage, we took in the scent of pine forest and went on alert the way horses do when they "smell the barn." We turned off Highway 83 at the sawmill at the edge of the small timber-and-recreation town of Seeley Lake and drove the old Forest Service road to the turnoff for the cabin at the north end of the lake. We pulled up in front of the cabin and my father cut the car's engine, which clicked as it cooled. All grew quiet. The giant western larch trees stood tall, silent, and stately in remembered places. Glimpses of the lake, silver and gunmetal blue, beckoned through the trees. The cabin had survived another winter. Unlocking and opening the cabin door released the familiar musk of the linseed oil and turpentine used to dress the logs. We were home.

ONE SPARKLING-BRIGHT MORNING at our cabin, my father and mother and I prepared for my first fishing trip. I was seven years old. Seeley Lake was unusually calm, the air still and the lake glassy, no neighbors around, no motorboats out on the water. The temperature was warm and the humidity low. Yet perfection is not a stable state. A few swirly clouds were visible to the north, but hopefully they would reduce glare on the water and improve the fishing. My mother fixed us a bag lunch, never mind that the creek my father and I were headed to was only a short hop from the cabin, and we could easily make it back by noon. Fishermen eat their lunch at the river. My mother placed the lunch bag on the steps in front of the kitchen alongside the fishing gear with the change of clothes we'd set out. A fisherman is responsible for his rod, reel, and flies, and if you forget one of the essentials, you do not deserve to fish, or so I've always been told. My mother smiled as she waved us on our way, but you could see a hint of worry in her eyes. There was an awful lot at stake. We three were in this together, and the fish, or at least one fish, had to cooperate.

Dad drove to a bridge over the creek and parked the car. A nearly impenetrable stand of willows grew on the banks and overhung the water, providing shade for trout, a habitat for insect life that fed the fish, and a formidable barrier for fishermen. The creek was one of several that act as a trout nursery for Seeley Lake. The big trout that had moved up-stream from the lake to spawn in the spring had gone back by now, leaving behind a crop of juvenile cutthroat and rainbow trout. By midsummer, a trout six inches long in this water was a whopper.

We crawled down the bank at the bridge, taking in the heavy scent of the sun-warmed creosote in the support timbers of the bridge, and waded down the middle of the creek to avoid the willow jungle. The creek ran nearly straight at first, too fast and shallow to hold trout. We waded on, entering an enclosed and welcoming world. The willows turned the creek into a tunnel with only a narrow wedge of sky above it, and in that channel flowed a second stream, a horizontal column of air made cool and humid by the riffling water below. The icy water bit through the worn cotton pants we used for fishing. My father and I held hands to keep our balance on the slippery stones lining the creek bed, which glistened as though they were emeralds, gold nuggets, and sapphires. We kicked up a few of the rocks, but the bottom was clean and we didn't raise the mud that would have warned the downstream trout of our approach.

After several hundred yards, the creek turned into a deep hole overhung with sheltering brush, a likely spot for a trout. Far downstream, though, in the narrow strip of sky visible above the creek, we saw what the enclosing brush had hidden from our sight until that moment—an abrupt line of dark, fast-moving storm clouds. The gathering wind made waves in the willows, flipping the slender leaves upside down and turning them from moss-green to a dusky sage color. My father looked at the darkening sky and the deep hole ahead and made a mental calculation.

"Okay," he said, "this is the place. Put a fly right there at the head of the riffle and let it drift down into the hole."

I unlimbered my rod, an old metal one with a bend or two in it, and I stripped out line and sent a fat wet fly sailing toward the top of the riffle. It took only a second before what had seemed to be a glossy stone in the creek bed transformed into a living thing: a trout. All six inches of it rose and took the fly, and even more magically in rising revealed a scarlet streak along its side. "Rainbow!" said my father. He leaned over me, his face alight with joy, eyes intent on the fish, and coached my every move. He so badly wanted me to catch that fish—and I did it. *My first trout. And it was a rainbow!*

The storm arrived in a great whoosh of wind. Sharp, icy pellets stung our faces. Hailstones rattled in the willows. With conditions deteriorating, we had to retreat quickly, but the bridge was an upstream slog and too far off. We headed ashore into the thick willows, figuring we could break through to the timbered ground above the bank. We plunged in, but I was a little kid and the spider web of rubbery roots and branches trapped my legs.

There was only one way to do this. My father removed his hat, put it on my head, hoisted me onto his shoulders, and took off through the brush like the halfback he'd once been. The hat came down over my face, and smelled of the oil and sweat. I grabbed fistfuls of his thick black hair. He yelped, but I held on, and then we both began to hoot and holler, and we busted through the willows and broke out into open ground on the bank high above the creek. He lifted me off his shoulders. As the hailstorm reached a fury, we ran and stumbled our way back to the car. We plopped into the front seat, ice balls dancing off us. We started to laugh and couldn't stop ourselves, grinning like a couple of slaphappy kids. Hail rattled harmlessly on the car's roof and piled up on the windshield.

The storm ended as quickly as it had begun. The sun popped out and the hailstones melted. It was only late morning and we weren't yet hungry, but we completed the ritual, eating our sandwiches, apples, and cookies in the car. My mother was surprised to see us come back so soon, but she couldn't have been happier when we told her, blow by blow, of the successful catch. She was bewildered, though, when we described the hailstorm, because the skies had been clear where she was, at the cabin. The sun shone there, bright as anything, all the rest of that glorious day.

LONG YEARS LATER, when my father had retired from teaching, taken up writing full time, and lived alone in Chicago as a widower, he wrote hopefully about the annual trip back to Montana, fishing, and the cabin. He wasn't up to writing individual letters that year, he noted in a Christmas letter to friends and family, but he still looked forward to another summer in Montana. "Jean and John, with their families, expect to be there for a few weeks at least sometime in the summer, and I am deeply touched. Seeley Lake is much more to me than the remnants of its scenery. When I am there I feel that my father, mother, and brother are also. It's a long way to come to view the clear cutting. Love has to bring all of us back."

CHAPTER TWO

UNSEEN POWER

THE REVEREND MACLEAN was almost certainly the first of the family on either side to become a fly-fisherman. According to my father, he did so because he thought it was his duty to take up the customs of his adopted homeland, leaving behind his Scottish and Canadian roots. By the time he took the pulpit in Missoula he had mostly shed his Scottish burr, but he still practiced to make his speech clear, rhythmic, and distinct. He often spoke his sermons out loud beforehand or even afterward, on occasion enlisting his sons as an audience. He would imitate the Greek orator Demosthenes, who rid himself of a speech impediment by putting pebbles in his mouth and repeating verses until he ran out of breath. The Reverend would stand on the shore of Seeley Lake with a mouthful of pebbles, speaking to the waters, as my father remembered—or perhaps as he imagined, mingling the ancient story with living memory. True or not, the anecdote well describes a man who built a reputation for eloquence and passed along to his descendants a taste for public speaking.

The Reverend Maclean was a stylish caster, wearing a glove, using lots of wrist, and working the rod in a four-count rhythm: back and pause for the line to straighten—two counts; forward and pause again for the line to extend—two more counts. And only then allow the fly to settle gracefully on the water. It's all in the twist of the wrist. That method is considered quaint today, or useful just for short casts, but it was the norm at the time and has a classic look when properly performed.

Modern casting does not follow these strict rules, but my grandfather was not a modern man. Gifted with his hands, he made his own flies out of whatever was available. He also invested in one of the finest fly rods ever made, an H. L. Leonard—the company's founder, Hiram Lewis Leonard, is regarded as the father of the American bamboo fly rod. The rod outlived him along with a fistful of "cabin rods" kept at the Seeley Lake cabin, where the Leonard went unnoticed for decades. Leonard bamboo rods were yellowish (rather than the common brown caused by being heated to make the bamboo stronger). My father had told me that the Reverend, and no one else in our family, had one. One day I spotted the three sections of a yellow rod amid the cluster of brown cabin rods. I had it authenticated as a Leonard rod, or at least the two lower sections. (The tip, it turned out, was a non-Leonard replacement. Broken tips were a regular occurrence with fly rods, and sporting goods stores had barrels of replacements at a buck per tip, take your choice.) Fly rods were left behind when my father departed Montana for the Midwest, but they were not forgotten. They were yet another link in the chain that bound the family to our home state.

MY PARENTS, NORMAN and Jessie, left Montana at a difficult time for anyone to start a new job and build a career, as they both set out to do. My father headed off to the University of Chicago on the eve of the Great Depression. He kept an arresting visual memory of what followed in those dark days, recalling how people gathered in anger and despair around a set of huge church bells awaiting installation in the university's Rockefeller Chapel, named for the school's Baptist founder and bankroller, John D. Rockefeller. The bells sat silent on the ground near the chapel tower and were reviled as a symbol of foolish extravagance in hard times. The university, though, had a heart. Facing a financial crisis and possible layoffs, the faculty voted itself a 10 percent pay cut, and no one lost a job. My mother followed my father to Chicago, found a job, and they married on September 24, 1931. Once past the Depression, and with time for starting a family running short, they had two children, my sister, Jean, and me, both born during the darkest days of World War II, Jean in 1942 and me the following year. The University of Chicago in those years was at the center of world-altering developments, among them fostering the atom bomb through the Manhattan Project and attempting to bridge the intellectual gulf between science and the arts. One can only imagine the impact Norman and Jessie, two handsome, high-spirited, and *fun* young people swinging in from what was still regarded as the Wild West, had on that hyperintelligent, somewhat cloistered community.

And yet Montana never lost its hold. Always there was a living, physical link binding us together. My father's family first came to Montana at the end of the nineteenth century when my grandfather, the Reverend Maclean, accompanied by his wife, Clara, took the pulpit at the First Presbyterian Church in Bozeman. The state of Montana in those days had the aura of a mythological kingdom, the place where a Big Sky hung over a land of scorching summers and endless winters. After the brief surge of mountain men and fur traders that followed Lewis and Clark, the state slowly became populated with more permanent homesteaders, miners, loggers, and cowboys, who for a long time barely outnumbered the grizzly bears and Indians.

The Reverend Maclean, who emigrated from Canada, went from pulpit to pulpit as preachers do until he was called to the First Presbyterian Church in Missoula in 1909. Accompanying him were Clara and their two sons, Norman and Paul, who had been born in Clarinda, Iowa, where the Reverend had served after leaving Bozeman. (My father was born on December 23, 1902, so close to Christmas he always wondered if his parents hadn't planned it that way.) Missoula became their hometown. The Reverend remained in the pulpit there for sixteen years until he was promoted to a senior administrative post in the church, which meant moving to Helena, the state capital. Once he completed that duty, he promptly moved back to Missoula, where he and Clara lived out their lives.

Norman and Paul fit in well with Missoula's rough-and-tumble ways, but they were preacher's kids and were heavily exposed to literature and learning. Norman led the way as the elder brother. He loved sports, was good at them, and throughout his life also enjoyed playing the role of Montana tough guy. He wrote poetry, read deeply, and consciously imitated his father, whose sermons could mesmerize a congregation. Norman would meet his buddies on Saturday nights on the steps of a bank building at Higgins Avenue and Main Street, an imposing Victorian structure made of large, rough-cut stones. The steps, framed by two marble columns, form a kind of speaker's platform. Standing between the columns, Norman would declaim Shakespeare and other literary lights to his friends, which earned him the nickname "Preacher."

My father was of medium height, just avoiding short, and his athletic body was thick and strong in the core, more like his dark-haired English mother than his tall, lean, red-haired Scottish father. In adulthood, he had deeply drawn facial features with what's called a "noble warrior" nose, and parted his thick black hair down the middle. Like others in the family then and now, he had a hard eye that came with a scowl. He made daily exercise a lifestyle, and maintained a weight of one hundred sixty-five pounds or close to it from the time he played halfback for Missoula County High School—memorably scoring the winning points against archrival Butte—through a long career as an English professor. A poem accompanying his high school yearbook entry reads:

They have joked so of his talking
I shan't even mention it,

For it's most with other talents
That he always makes a hit.

Norman worked on backcountry crews for the Forest Service in summers starting at age fifteen, when World War I drained the woods of manpower. Later, those summers helped pay for an elite education at Dartmouth College. He cleared and built trails, fought fires, and worked hard enough to lose twenty to twenty-five pounds in a summer: he'd come home at the end of the season skinny and shaggy haired. At Dartmouth, he earned another nickname, "Bull Montana," after a popular movie figure of the day, that fit his determined attitude. He also attended poet Robert Frost's writing seminar, which he called "Frost on Frost," held in the basement of the chairman of the English department's house. "He talked straight to you, and often poetry was there, or something close to it," said Norman. The great poet would enter the seminar room at the minute the class was to begin and immediately commence speaking about his work. Frost would walk in circles in front of a big fireplace as he continued to talk, and as the end of the class drew near, he'd edge toward the exit—and shut the door behind him on his final word at the final minute. "He wasn't interested in the thoughts of undergraduates," my father reported.

Norman told a gentler story about Frost's most famous poem, "Stopping by Woods on a Snowy Evening," written in 1922 at the time my father was taking the seminar. Frost would later claim he wrote the poem "in just a few minutes without strain." But that's not the story he told the students, according to my father. Frost related a struggle with the poem's concluding line. Until that point in the poem, each four-line stanza had a strict rhyme scheme, AABA, until the final stanza, which follows an AAA rhyme scheme and lacked a final line. Frost told the class how he had walked out into his garden repeating the third line of the unfinished stanza over and over, "and miles to go before I sleep," searching for a follow-on line, until he realized he already had it. The simple repetition of that line at the poem's conclusion has charmed poetry lovers ever since.

Upon graduation from Dartmouth, Norman was invited to stay on and teach English. He did so for two years until his father told him he'd stopped growing and had fallen into a rut. He sent in a notice to Dartmouth and applied for a high school teaching job in Montana, but state education authorities turned him down on the grounds that he lacked education credits, despite his college teaching experience. Infuriated, he never forgot the insult and within months had left the state.

My mother, Jessie Burns, came from the aforementioned Wolf Creek, a tiny town stuck off in a canyon a ways north of the state capital of Helena. The canyon was just wide enough to accommodate Wolf Creek's two streets, plus a railroad line and a prized trout stream, Little Prickly Pear Creek. Jessie was tall, thin, and freckled. She was a tomboy in her youth, proud of her nicknames "Jake" or "Jakie," and had a bob hairstyle. She later reverted to Jessie and let her rich auburn hair grow nearly to her waist, and, by all accounts, became a stunner. My father began his letters to her with "Lovely Jessie," and sometimes ended them the same way.

They had met under romantic circumstances, at a party out in the Helena valley one December. They were returning home in Jessie's car with another couple when a blizzard caught them and the car's radiator froze up. Norman poured in more water, but it, too, froze. He then set out in the storm to hike into town for help, but on his way back to the stranded vehicle it came puttering along toward him. The radiator was still frozen, but it was so cold that the engine didn't overheat. Norman felt foolish, but Jessie remembered him as the hero of the blizzard.

Her hometown of Wolf Creek had a one-room schoolhouse with several disadvantages: it ran only to the eighth grade, and it often washed away in spring floods. Jessie longed for life on a broader canvas. Happily, her father, John Henry Burns, who owned Wolf Creek's general store, went about educating his children in Helena. He bought a handsome Victorian house in the capital city for his seven children to live in while they attended school there. His wife, Florence, and all the children are recorded in the 1930 U.S. census as living in Helena. John stayed on in Wolf Creek tending the store, but he hated being apart from his family and Florence frequently remained there with him. Jessie, the eldest child, was often left in sole charge of the Helena operation, which she ran with a loose but loving hand, the hallmark of her future as a mother and an administrator. She carried a lot of responsibility, but she was no goody-goody: her high school yearbook had a note next to her picture: "To make a disturbance is to be happy." She had what my father called "swish," meaning style with a flair.

She wound up working for more than thirty years for the University of Chicago, for seventeen of those years as executive secretary of the Medical & Biological Sciences Alumni Association. She built up the organization, publishing an alumni bulletin, organizing an annual alumni dinner, and arranging other social and fundraising activities for alumni around the country. She had a tiny office next to the medical students' lounge and locker room, where residents often slept on couches between long rounds. She always had an open door and a pack of cigarettes close to hand, available to bewildered and distressed students—and faculty. "Jessie knew what was to be said," remarked Dr. Sidney Schulman, a distinguished neurologist, and one of her best friends. "She said less than she knew, but she said enough, and she said it with humor, with literary allusions, and with simplicity. She came to be a sort of housemother. In being this, she was unaware of it—no self-satisfied awareness that what she was doing was noble. She was not playacting. It was part of her existence."

She empathized with people from all walks of life, a trait that could come in a rush so sudden and overpowering that it took your breath away. She hadn't finished college, but venerable scholars from the university came to her little office to pour out their troubles. Women with medical and other advanced degrees, relegated by gender discrimination to the second ranks of science, gathered around her for comradeship and support. Upon retirement, she was given the Gold Key Award for Distinguished Service by the Alumni Association, the first and only time this award has been presented to someone who was not a physician, biologist, or graduate of the school. The cigarettes would win in the end, however. Too soon, she would make a final journey to Montana to a hill overlooking Wolf Creek that her family had called Mount Jessie when she was young.

———

HOW DID WE ever become a fishing family? We certainly didn't descend from the landed gentry who sport fished in Scotland, England, and Ireland, the lands whence we'd come. It's likely that no one in the Maclean or Burns families picked up a fly rod until they arrived in Montana. The Macleans hailed from the tiny Isle of Coll, one of the Inner Hebrides located about seven miles west of the Clan Maclean stronghold, the Isle of Mull. Laughlan Maclean, a carpenter by trade, emigrated from Coll to Nova Scotia in 1821 with his wife, Elizabeth Campbell, and family documents record that they made the last stages of the long journey in an open boat, from Cape Breton to Pictou, and then by foot to Cape John, another sixteen miles away. John Norman Maclean was born in Marshy Hope, Pictou County, Nova Scotia, on July 28, 1882, to Laughlan's son Norman and his wife, Mary MacDonald, both of whom were born in Nova Scotia. The couple had ten children, far too many to be supported as adults by the family farm. John, the second son, showed academic promise and attended Pictou Academy, a private secondary school of renown in the coastal fishing community of Pictou.

The academy, started as a nondenominational Christian training ground for ministers, offered a remarkable education for its time and purpose, one strong in science as well as the classics, and it had a lasting influence on John. "The Pictou Academy originated among men of the most liberal sentiment, and whose strongest opinion was that knowledge should be free as the light of Heaven," declares a resolution passed in 1827 by the school's trustees. Dr. Thomas McCulloch, a Presbyterian minister, founded the school and modeled it on the University of Glasgow, a world center of scientific learning. Dr. McCulloch gathered a collection of insects and birds for a natural history museum that was significant enough to attract John James Audubon on his return from an expedition to Labrador in 1833. When Audubon pronounced it a "fine collection" and noted that it held specimens he lacked, Dr. McCulloch generously opened his cases and passed along a few.

John's name appears in the Pictou Academy records as J. N. McLean of Glenbard. Like many Scots' names, the spelling of Maclean is irregular; it appears as McLean, Maclean, and MacLean in various official and unofficial records. The school offered a rich assortment of courses in English language and literature; French, German, Greek, and Latin; as well as physics, mathematics, geology, and practical botany. John's devotion to the life of the spirit and love for the natural world, nurtured at the academy, marked not only his preaching but future generations of his family, and would be echoed in the opening line of *A River Runs through It,* "In our family, there was no clear line between religion and fly fishing."

John attended Dalhousie College in Halifax, Nova Scotia, and then headed west to Manitoba for health reasons, perhaps seeking a drier climate in the flattish prairies of the northern Great Plains than that of damp, maritime Nova Scotia. At Manitoba College in Winnipeg, before he graduated, he spent summers at "missionary work," riding a circuit to small, remote congregations in the province. He lived for a time next door to two sisters from the family of John Davidson, the first settler in the New Haven district north of Manitou, Manitoba. One of those sisters was Clara Davidson, the future Mrs. Maclean.

John Davidson was an energetic and enterprising figure. He settled first with his family in Quebec, but finding the land poor he moved on and homesteaded in Manitoba, making the final journey by oxcart. He was a wheat farmer and his carpentry skills were much in demand for barn raisings and other projects. Considered a leader of the pioneer community, he helped build a log cabin that served as both a school and a church for Presbyterian services—the Davidsons originally came from northern England near the Scottish border and were Presbyterians. A cultured man for his time, John Davidson played the violin until an accident with a saw deprived him of several fingers. He believed in educating his children—even his daughters, up to a point.

He gave each of his four sons $2,000 to pursue advanced studies, and two of them became doctors, one having been inspired by watching a doctor stitch up his father's saw-torn hand. A third went on to become a mayor of Manitou. When Clara and the other daughters also showed intellectual promise, he did not turn his back.

"The girls did not want to help at home and then get married, as most pioneer girls were expected to do," the Manitou history records. "They wanted further education and persuaded their father to find a place for them in Manitou. They finished their education and became teachers. Clara taught at the Mowbray school, near the United States border, in 1889." She was just seventeen.

John Maclean was ten years older than Clara, but they shared a love of learning and the Presbyterian Church, and rode the Sunday circuit together during their courtship. In 1893, he completed advanced studies at San Francisco Theological Seminary in San Anselmo, California, and was ordained as a minister. They married on August 1 of that year in Pembina, Manitoba, according to the Manitoba marriage index, and the couple then returned to California. He served as pastor in Vacaville, California, until 1897, when he traveled for the first time to Montana, where he became pastor of the First Presbyterian Church in Bozeman.

The young minister and Clara arrived in Bozeman during the twenty-fifth anniversary year of the founding of the church. At the anniversary celebration, Mrs. Melinda Rich, a charter member of the congregation, painted a verbal picture of life in Bozeman a quarter century earlier. Mule trains, ox trains, and emigrant wagons mixed with cowboys and saddle horses; stagecoaches were eagerly awaited with hopes of letters from "all the dear ones left behind." Indians passed through town, with chiefs leading the way and dismounting to visit the stores. That picture isn't far off from my father's description of Missoula during the family's first years there, when the Flathead set up teepees along the Clark Fork in summer, main streets were built wide enough for a wagon and a team of horses to turn around—today's Stephens Avenue is a broad reminder— saloons prospered and the population included a very rough element.

During Reverend Maclean's five years in Bozeman, he helped set up a committee to erect a new church building, as he would again in Missoula. He and Clara then left Bozeman for the Westminster Presbyterian Church in Clarinda, in southwest Iowa, as noted earlier, where he took the pulpit in 1902. They stayed there for seven years.

The First Presbyterian Church in Missoula contacted the Reverend with an opening as pastor in January 1909, after two other ministers not only turned down the job but refused even to visit the frontier town. The church elders did not lose hope. "After due deliberation it was decided the clerk should open correspondence with the Rev. J. N. McLean [*sic*] of Clarinda, Iowa, and write him to visit our guild with a view to becoming pastor of this church," the minutes report. The Reverend Maclean did not hesitate. Within weeks, he answered the call, packed up wife and sons, and returned to the state that would be his home for the rest of his life. The family boarded the Northern Pacific's fabled North Coast Limited train, the premier streamliner that ran from Chicago to Seattle and Portland. (Today's Empire Builder making the same connection takes a northerly route that misses Missoula.) They arrived in Missoula on February 26, 1909. The Reverend was given a sterling send-off by the Clarinda *Herald*, which said the city was losing "a scholar and a thinker of great ability . . . He is not pretentious; he is sincere and sympathetic and patient with the process of truth."

The Reverend Maclean was a fine scholar who read the Bible in Greek for pleasure as well as devotion. He'd been reared on a farm, however, and after he took the pulpit in Missoula, he still helped feed his young family with rod and gun. And not just his family. "Dr. and Mrs. J. N. Maclean treated some of their friends to venison dinners Monday and Tuesday evenings," the *Missoulian* newspaper reported in November 1913. "The game was brought in last week from Rock Creek, the result of Dr. Maclean's good marksmanship." Mrs. Maclean added grace to the game dinner by setting a table "made beautiful with kinnikinnick berries and red shaded candles," and organizing a musical performance at the end of the evening.

Of my grandmother, the church's session notes record that "the wife of the pastor has exerted a mighty power for good in this church and community," and they listed among her virtues that she was "capable, tactful, loving and tireless." One First Presbyterian document calls her "rarely gifted" and a near equal partner of the pastor. "Though not officially so designated, Mrs. Maclean has been an assistant pastor and social worker of striking ability." She brought gentility to the frontier.

My sister and I called her Granny, and she spent several weeks with us each summer at the cabin. She and my mother would jockey for dominance over the iron cook-stove in the cabin's kitchen, in which my father would build a wood fire each morning. But she was the leader without peer when we went huckleberry picking because she knew the hot spots, the places where she could sit without moving and "pick a pie." Granny joined us at the cabin until her health no longer permitted it. She was cared for in her last years by a neighboring family who were longtime family friends, the Turrells. I wrote this note to an old friend about an incident involving Granny and Joe Turrell, that family's patriarch, when she was at her best.

My father and Joe Turrell and I went fishing one time. We caught a bunch of fish, which we carefully counted, but somehow one of the fish was lost in the upholstery of Joe's car. After he dropped us off at the cabin, my father, mother, sister, Granny, and I were standing on the steps waving goodbye as he pulled away when I shouted, "Sure hope you find that goddamned fish!" I had no idea I'd said anything wrong, but of course the remark stopped the show. Joe hurriedly drove off. My father blanched. Granny's face became stormy. My mother looked to the heavens. As soon as Joe was out of sight my father started giving me the devil. But Granny looked him hard in the eye and remarked, "Well, Norman, where do you suppose he learned to say that?" I loved Granny a lot. But I loved her a lot more after that one.

ON MY MOTHER'S SIDE of the family, her father (yet another John) was not really a sporting man. John Burns was born in Marlborough, Massachusetts, on January 24, 1873, a few years after his family settled there. According to family lore, supported by a DNA trace, they came from Northern Ireland in or near Belfast, where they had been shopkeepers. John's father owned a stone quarry in Massachusetts, but while John was still a child, his father traded the quarry for one in Eau Claire, Wisconsin. He made the swap sight unseen, and it turned out to be a dud. The Burns children were sent off at early ages to make their own way in the world. About the age of twelve John was dispatched up to British Columbia, Canada, to help an older brother, Tom, who had a mining claim near Kootenay Lake, not far from the Idaho border. The first winter Tom set out in a rowboat with all the money they had to get supplies at a town on the other side of the long and narrow lake. Rowing over was a calculated risk and Tom lost. On the way back, a storm came roaring down the narrows containing the lake, which acted as a funnel and accelerated the wind flow. The boat capsized and Tom drowned, along with the supplies and whatever was left of their funds. The other miners helped young John get through the winter, and after the ice went out in the spring he traded the mining claim for a rooming house in a town on the other side of the lake. His sister Kate joined him there to help with the business, and the two forged a lasting bond.

About 1890 the siblings made their way to Butte, Montana, then "the richest hill on earth." First gold and silver and then copper accounted for Butte's enormous, if brief, wealth and importance. John did not take to mining. He started a grocery, but business was slow and as a supplement he gave dancing lessons at the Old Miners' Union

Hall in Philipsburg near Butte. When both businesses took off, he gave up the dancing lessons, but he held on to the notion that workingmen needed a healthy activity for leisure time and were willing to pay for it. The move to Wolf Creek came in 1904 when John and Kate's husband, Sam Arthur, heard that the town's general store had come up in an estate sale. They took loans from friends to put the purchase together. That same year John married his sweetheart, Florence McLeod, who had emigrated from Canada and worked in the post office in Granite near Phillipsburg, a mining town that was abandoned and today is a ghost town.

John took up his place behind the counter at the Arthur and Burns General Store in Wolf Creek selling everything from hard candy to hard-rock mining supplies. My mother, Jessie, was the first of the seven children, arriving January 24, 1905. Jessie was born in Butte, where Sam and Kate ran another enterprise, a boardinghouse, and Kate acted as midwife. After five years Sam, restless as was his nature—and perhaps tired of traveling between Butte and Wolf Creek—asked to be bought out of the Wolf Creek store for the round sum of $10,000. This was only a few years after miners struck for $4 a day, and that $10,000 represented about ten years of a workingman's salary. John raised the sum, though, and took over the store; Sam had second thoughts years later, but a deal was a deal. When Little Prickly Pear Creek washed the store away in a flood one spring, John rebuilt it in a "safer" spot—right across the street, the narrow canyon offering few options. The building has survived as a restaurant and bar.

The fortunes of the enterprise rose high and fell low in rhythm with those of Wolf Creek. The economic mainstay down through the years was the big ranches in the Dearborn River country to the north, the reason the town was created in the first place. The Great Northern Railroad wanted a railhead for the sheep and cattle produced by the ranches, so it ran a spur to Wolf Creek off the Shelby-Butte line. In the town's greater days, the ranchers drove their herds and flocks down from the Dearborn country through the narrow gap cut by Wolf Creek, which joins the larger Little Prickly Pear Creek on the edge of the town. Cattle and sheep came milling and bawling down the main street and on to the railhead. The ranchers stocked up at Burns' General Merchandise, the name adopted after the split with Arthur, buying months' worth of supplies at a crack before heading home.

In 1935, the building of a good road running through Wolf Creek from Great Falls to Helena signaled the end of the town's importance as a stage point. With Helena only thirty-six miles away on a paved highway, it became more convenient for locals to go there for supplies. Even so, a substantial number kept their custom with John Burns. And he had a rancher friend in the Dearborn River country who thought the world of him, and when the store hit hard times, John would drive to the ranch, return with a check, and carry on. He in his turn supported the community. On nothing more than a handshake, he'd often grubstake a prospector searching the nearby hills for ore. Not much ore was ever found, and many debts went unpaid. The hills around Wolf Creek are still pockmarked with failed workings from those days. A photo Norman took of John late in his life, though, shows him smiling to himself, a halo of curly white hair around his head. "We all loved Dad," Jessie often said.

OUR FISHING SEASON most always began in Wolf Creek, where we stopped at the Burns homestead to recover from the overland journey. Ken and Dottie had built a new house, but the old home was right next door, a bit faded, and that's where we stayed. John Burns had liked his luxuries, and one of them was an extra-long bathtub carted up from Helena and installed with a water heater, big enough for only one tubful. We kids could practically swim in the tub, but about the third cousin in a row to be bathed on a Saturday night wound up with a quick dip in the gray, tepid water.

Little Prickly Pear Creek was good fishing even where it ran through town. In the narrow canyon outside town, the creek meandered in curlicues in a greenbelt of willows and cottonwood trees, and the resin hung in the air with a pungent, coming-home fragrance. In the spring large rainbow trout would come up from the Missouri River to spawn, and in summer, after the big fish had gone back to the Missouri, the creek was still loaded with a permanent population of nice-sized trout. If we arrived early enough in the year, the large rainbows were still there, and my dad would go out and delight everyone by coming back at dark with a basketful. When I was bigger, I could walk out of the house to the creek and reliably catch a limit. When my dad, my uncle Ken, his son Bob, and I went out together, only a short distance from town, we would all limit up in a couple of hours, and the protein was always welcome.

One summer we went on an elaborate family trip far into the Dearborn River country. Relatives gathered from as far away as California as well as the Midwest. We loaded up Old Faithful, Ken's rugged black pickup. It had air-conditioning: a little fan with leather paddles mounted in the cab to stir the air. We put mattresses in the truck bed to cushion the ride and piled in camping gear and a big metal tub filled with ice and bottled beer. We had to cross the Dearborn River many times on the dirt road, not much more than a track in places. Each crossing became jollier. The men would hop out, move rocks around in the creek bed, and push Old Faithful across and up the bank on the far side, fortifying themselves with the beer before, during, and after the crossing. Someone had brought a bottle of stronger stuff that was passed on the sly from hand to hand.

We arrived at the chosen site and set up our camp. The men went fishing, but along toward evening the weather worsened and a cold front came in with a few flakes of snow—this was Montana, after all, where it could and often did snow in any month of the year. By morning the washbasins would have a skim of ice. The mattresses had been laid out side by side in the tent, and we little ones had just been bedded down with warm blankets, snug and drowsy, when all hell broke loose. In a moment we were wide awake and scared. Outside we heard rumbling, snorts, and crashes. My mother and the aunts dashed into the tent and one said to me, "Come out and see your father!"

We piled out of the tent to a scene of mad chaos. Cattle pounded through the campsite, snorting clouds of vapor that hung suspended in the frigid air. Thick heads, eyes filled with terror, swung wildly back and forth as they scattered pots and pans and knocked over chairs and tables. Behind them out of the woods came hard-riding cowboys spurring their horses, swinging quirts, and hollering to drive the cattle. Their leader yanked his horse to a halt in front of the tent, a larger-than-life figure right out of a Charlie Russell painting. He wore leather chaps, gloves and cuffs, a broad western hat pulled down tight, a scarlet bandanna, and most impressive to the young male eye, he had a leather scabbard rigged to his saddle *with a rifle sticking out of it*.

He was furious.

"What the hell are you doing here?" he shouted as his horse shifted, tossing its head.

My dad stood, quietly but firmly. A man on a horse always has it over one on the ground, but steadiness under pressure was my father's particular strength. My father was hatless, carried no weapon, and was modestly dressed. He raised his voice just loud enough to be heard. He told the man on the horse that we had asked for and received permission from the ranch owner to be where we were. We were a Wolf Creek family, not trespassers or poachers. The uncles, arrayed behind him, backed him up like a chorus, nodding their heads, repeating "Burns, we're the Burns family!" and calling out the name of the rancher who had given his permission. It came out that the rancher was the brother of the man on the horse.

"Well, nobody told me that!" the cowboy yelled, sounding petulant.

The raging cattle had vanished. The horseman was

alone now and knew he had lost the moral high ground. "To hell with this, I've got to catch up with my cattle!" he shouted. He put the spurs to his horse and galloped off into the timber.

Our stays in Wolf Creek after the long drive west and trips to the Dearborn River weren't always so dramatic. But the Dearborn River backcountry was always a wild and remote place, and we went there many times in Old Faithful to camp, picnic, and fish. The road to the Dearborn runs along the foothills of the Rocky Mountains, a land of long vistas punctuated by square buttes that was once home to the buffalo and Native American tribes who hunted them. From the road, you can see out to the enormous eroded breaks that hold the north-flowing Missouri River. If we passed another vehicle it was an event. Coming home late from a trip to the Dearborn, we'd lie on the mattresses in the back of the pickup and try to count the stars, singing old songs like "Home on the Range" or "Bury Me Not on the Lone Prairie" until we nodded off. The road's been designated Highway 434 and paved since then, but it's still a lonesome drive, punctuated by occasional ranch buildings near water courses, grazing cattle, and all by itself and not locked, a one-room community church and adjoining cemetery.

CHAPTER THREE

WHEN THE MOUNTAINS ROARED

WHEN WE FINALLY arrived at the cabin at Seeley Lake at the end of our cross-country trek, Jean and I would rush inside to open drawers and check bookshelves and cupboards to make sure the household goods, books, fishing gear, toys, and other objects we'd squirreled away the previous season were right where we'd left them. We didn't have much there, but we valued everything we had. In rummaging a dresser drawer I once found a hidden treasure, a faded red-and-black-checked shirt pushed back into a forgotten corner. I put it on. The shoulders hung off to the sides, but it looked like it had a history and I tucked it deep into my jeans to make it fit.

"That was my brother's shirt," my father said. "He had broad shoulders." From then on, it became my everyday shirt, a link to the family's legendary master fisherman, Paul, my missing uncle and my father's younger brother. It took years for my father to explain—and for me to understand—why Paul was nowhere to be found in person when he was so strongly present with us in spirit. The first explanation, offered without detail, was bewildering to young ears: "He was murdered."

My family did not discuss its problems in an easy and open manner, although we all tried at different times, in our own ways. My father was pleased at first when I adopted Paul's red-and-black-checked shirt, but I finally wore it see-through thin, with holes and tears, and my mother insisted it be thrown away. I was sad to see it go, but the loss angered my father, and that reaction, too, has taken decades to understand. Like the fallen smokejumpers my father later would write about, Paul was young when he died, did not leave much behind, and needed someone to remember him.

Mystery always clung to Paul, even regarding the basics of his biography. There is no birth certificate or even baptismal record for him as there is for Norman, and his year of birth was long in doubt. (James R. Hepworth, a retired English professor and dedicated fisherman, eventually dug out the answer from a Clarinda newspaper clipping: November 4, 1905.) Diligent research by many people over a span of years has nailed down how long Paul studied at the University of Montana and then at Dartmouth College, where he followed Norman and from where he graduated. Some answers, though, are forever beyond reach. To this day, conflicting stories and wild rumors abound concerning the circumstances of his death, not at Lolo Hot Springs nor elsewhere in Montana as portrayed in Robert Redford's movie adaptation of *A River Runs through It*, but in a dark alley on a Sunday night after he had joined his brother Norman in Chicago.

Paul had first become a presence for me through the red-and-black-checked shirt, but the effect lingered and grew as my life followed parallel paths to his as a fisherman and journalist. When I was young, I heard the family stories about Paul, in carefully edited bursts, but in later years I collected anecdotes and impressions from others who had known him, too. As a Chicago newspaper reporter with access to files and reports—special access in some cases, because in time I became his closest living relative—I looked carefully into what can be known about his life and death. And for that matter, what can never be known. There are few surviving physical artifacts from his life. A well-preserved bamboo rod that Paul almost certainly used. A pewter beer mug from his time at Dartmouth etched with "Paul" Maclean and his final year there, 1928. The picture of him that emerged over time leaves just enough room for the movie's version of Paul, memorably played by a young Brad Pitt: the charming but tarnished hero whose inevitable fall comes more from birth and circumstance—a "vicious mole of nature," as Shakespeare put it—than from choice. But facts are facts. The account that follows is based on conversations over many decades and records and other documents that go back more than a century. Some of the stories are new, some are funny and full of life, and some are not very pretty. But they all lead in the same direction and ultimately to the same end.

THE MACLEAN BROTHERS were unusually close. Three years apart, they excelled at athletics, fishing in particular. Both were drawn to the study and practice of the written word. A photo taken just after the family moved to Missoula shows the two boys together in wintertime on a slushy downtown street. Mount Sentinel looms in the not-so-distant background. The handsome Montana Building, with its ornamental cornices, stands at the intersection; overhead are cables to power the town's new streetcar system; and along the street are a few carriage-like versions of the automobile. The photo is such an icon of "old Missoula" that it was made into a popular postcard. The scene is little changed today, except the cars are modern, a welter of traffic lights has replaced the streetcar power lines, and the Montana Building, while still there, has been stripped of its ornamental cornices.

The boys look directly at the camera, hold hands, and boast a similar, almost defiant expression: us against the universe! Norman is bigger, but their physical difference would not endure—Paul in adulthood was about a half inch shorter but fifteen pounds heavier than Norman. Norman, though, would always be the big brother, forever holding his little brother's hand. Norman would marry, raise a family, and succeed as a teacher of English at an academic institution that stressed science and research. He kept the Seeley Lake cabin in family hands, and in his seventh decade achieved a lifetime ambition by writing and publishing *A River Runs through It,* which at long last told his brother's story.

MY FATHER TOLD me there were three things to remember about our corner of Montana: timber, fishing, and fire. In 1910, the year after the family arrived in Missoula, the signature wildland fire of the twentieth century—the Big Burn—tested the new minister at the First Presbyterian Church. The fire season appeared to be nearing a successful conclusion late that August after a long dry spell when a heavy windstorm from the Pacific roared across the Northwest, fanning numerous small fires that had been nearly out into a raging multistate inferno. An enormous cloud of smoke and soot blanketed northwestern Montana and the panhandle of Idaho, stretching east to New England and even halfway across the Atlantic Ocean to Greenland. The Big Burn killed more than four score firefighters. The exact number remains uncertain: only twenty-nine bodies could be identified well enough to send next of kin their remains and wages due. Many of the others are buried in St. Maries, Idaho, under stones marked "Unknown." The fires of 1910 stood as the greatest loss of life from a wildfire for over a century, until eighty-five civilians were killed in Northern California's Camp Fire in 2018, with one more still listed as missing.

Missoula was the epicenter of the battle, covered by smoke so dense the streetlamps had to be turned on during daytime hours. The railyard became the staging point for firefighters, who were recruited wherever men could be found, famously from saloons. Men, horses, and supplies were loaded onto railroad cars and sent off to fight the fires. Supervisors considered themselves lucky if their men had sobered up by the time they bent to dig a fire line. Elers Koch, a Forest Service supervisor in Missoula and a principal organizer of the battle, memorably called it the time "when the mountains roared." The Forest Service, organized only five years earlier, found itself overwhelmed. Koch, a Forest Service man from hat to boots, called the firefight "a complete defeat for the newly organized Forest Service forces." In future years, he worked to make the agency into a great firefighting machine yet lost an epic battle to take a tolerant view of fire in the wild. His "let burn" advocacy for some fires would not be vindicated until modern times. Koch became a neighbor of ours at Seeley Lake, a family friend, and toward the end of his life an almost mystical presence.

With flames, death, and furious dark clouds all around, the elders of the First Presbyterian Church in Missoula sought out their new pastor, some fearing the end times had arrived, or so the story is told. They found the Maclean family all camped on an island at a fork of the Bitterroot River, on a fishing trip. An impromptu rescue party waded from the bank to the island, crossed hands, and carried mother Clara and four-year-old Paul to safety. Norman and his father took each other's hands, held on to their fishing rods, and waded back to the bank. The Reverend Maclean, Norman later recounted, assumed the role of patriarch and assured his parishioners the world was not coming to its biblical conclusion. He told them to go back to their homes, and they did.

—

BACK IN MISSOULA in calmer times, with the Big Burn behind them, Norman and Paul were homeschooled by their parents, a daunting experience for all concerned. Clara, who had been a schoolteacher, instructed them in the morning for several hours, then sent them along to their father to recite lessons and submit exercises, which were then rewritten and rewritten, each version shorter and tighter, much like in the movie. "Never be too proud to cut a single word!" the father told his sons. The drills standing before the Reverend were short but intense, which may help explain why it took Norman until his seventies to produce a full-length book. "I can't tell you how many lifetimes a fifteen-minute period can be when you're six, seven, eight, nine and ten and a half and you are in the room with a redheaded Presbyterian minister who knows the answers," Norman said.

The Reverend drummed lessons into the boys, but none was delivered more forcefully than the exhortation, "Do something great!" What that "something" might be was for them to discover. He told his parishioners the same, that it was their duty to God and to themselves to rise up and achieve greatness. The intensity comes through in reported remarks he made a year after arriving in Missoula, when his former congregation at the First Presbyterian Church in Bozeman invited him back for the grand opening of the new church building he'd helped to plan. Taking his family with him, he boarded a train and traveled to Bozeman. "Expect great things from God," he told the gathering there. "But expectation is not all. We must *attempt* great things for God. Great Things! *Great Things!*" The words *great, greater,* and *greatest* appear fifteen times in that one brief address. (The pulpit from which he preached was moved many decades later to Livingston, where it was used in church scenes for the movie *A River Runs Through It*.)

Once the truant officer had had his way, Norman and Paul went to public schools, where they found early success. At Missoula County High School, both played on the school football team, worked on the *Konah,* the school newspaper—Norman as business manager, Paul as features editor—and racked up other accomplishments. "We just found out this year that Paul is such a star in basketball," enthused the 1923 *Bitter Root*, the senior publication for his graduation year. A separate yearbook for 1923 noted "Polly" was the "best blocker on the team this year, never failing to get his man on every play." Paul's activities included dramatic club, junior class vice president, first place in the Dixon Declamation contest, staff on the *Bitter Root* yearbook, and vice president of the Latin Club. He also won acclaim for his efforts for the Carnival, an annual evening of plays, stunts, and other programs put on by students.

None of the brothers' achievements, however, was so fully described in school publications as Norman's role in "the triumph of the season," as the 1920 *Bitter Root* called Missoula's football victory over archrival Butte. That game won for Missoula the title of Western Montana Champions. "A determined team went to Butte," the *Bitter Root* reported. "The field was very muddy, but nothing could stop the smashing attack. . . . Maclean played star football at the halfback position." The game was scoreless into the fourth quarter, but in the waning minutes Missoula launched a final, relentless drive. Maclean was described as a "hard boy . . . a fast man, good at forward passing." The ball inside the opponent's twenty-yard line, this was his moment. "With every player poised and doing his best, Maclean carried the ball another 19 yards for the touchdown." That was the first and last score of the game. Missoula 6, Butte 0. "From the demonstration given by the students upon the team's return one could gather what an event it was," the *Bitter Root* wrote.

Paul's own gridiron heroics playing halfback made exciting reading two years later in the *Missoulian* account of a "smashing" offense—which led Missoula to a crushing 59–3 victory over its rival Helena. Paul, "shooting through center for heavy yardage," ran for two of the home team's nine touchdowns. On the last drive of the game, he took the ball "to within three feet of the goal" before the final gun ended the embarrassment.

Being football heroes gave Norman and Paul a dose of local fame, but their future lives depended on getting a solid literary education. The Reverend Maclean had provided the inspiration and early training. At Missoula County High School, Norman encountered another formidable mentor, the head of the school's English department, Miss Mabel Irene Rich. Her book, *A Study of the Types of Literature*, was a standard text for decades in high schools across the nation. Miss Rich instructed Norman, as he remarked in *A River Runs through It,* never to say anything was "more perfect," because a perfect thing cannot be more so. He disputes that remark in the book, and he regularly challenged her in person. "Norman kept Miss Rich continuously amused in her sixth-period English class by arguing with her," the *Bitter Root* senior publication noted. "Now since he is going to leave the M. H. S., 'Preacher' has graciously offered to teach some daring young Junior the Art of Contradicting your English Teacher Tactfully." Miss Rich, though, had the last word. In her *Study*, she wrote, and surely taught, "Lyric poetry is the utterance of the human heart in poetic form," and her former pupil took that elegant remark to his own heart. The title story in *A River Runs through It*, brief at a hundred four pages, meets in its own way her definition of what a lyric poem must be: "sincere, spontaneous, and express strong emotion . . . It is usually very short."

Miss Rich also taught Shakespeare, Norman's favorite author. He especially favored the tragedies, which Miss Rich described as plays in which the hero "must die by the law of his own sin whether it is one of commission or omission." That harsh thought is never articulated and applied to Paul in *A River*, but the idea is there, in the undercurrent of inevitable destruction that drives the narrative.

Norman did not name Miss Rich in *A River*, but her influence on him was profound. A June 1935 article in the *Missoulian* newspaper about an event honoring Miss Rich upon her retirement noted her "national renown" and reported an anecdote about an unnamed former student. While attending a "large middle western university," as Norman did, the student went with friends to a performance of Shakespeare's *Macbeth*, and on the way home began describing what he had seen in the play. "But we did not see all that," one of the friends remarked. "No, you wouldn't," came the tart reply, "for you never studied Shakespeare with Miss Rich."

Camping, fishing, schoolwork, and daily prayer, including on bended knees next to the family dining table before meals, marked the boys early teenage years—and church sometimes twice on Sundays. Also fighting. They took punches at each other until a stray blow of Paul's landed on their mother, who was trying to separate them. The boys found plenty of that action around Missoula, where in a town of loggers, railroaders, and woodsmen fistfighting was considered a kind of field sport and a fitting end to a boisterous Saturday night. Norman gave it up in good time, but Paul into adulthood was noted for never walking away from a fight—and for provoking one on occasion.

The brothers at first went separate ways for college. After considering other institutions—among them Harvard and Washington & Jefferson College near Pittsburgh—Norman headed for Dartmouth College in Hanover, New Hampshire, in 1920. "I thought I would be happier at the Indian school," he said.

Dartmouth's motto is *Vox Clamantis in Deserto*, which the college translates as "a voice crying in the wilderness." The phrase, from Isaiah 40:3, states the original purpose of Dartmouth, to evangelize Indians, but it could justly be applied to the boy from the Montana backcountry. The school graduated only nineteen Native Americans in its first two hundred years of existence, dating from 1769. But in 1970 it began a recruiting program and since then more than seven hundred Native Americans have attended, an example of the power of legacy, even one long neglected.

Today, Dartmouth's Native American Program is a beacon for promising students from tribes in Montana and elsewhere.

Norman was diligent in his studies, learned to play the Eastern sport of handball, and was active in the Beta Theta Pi fraternity. He also was "tapped" to join the Sphinx, one of Dartmouth's secret and exclusive senior societies, and proudly carried the society's emblematic walking stick with an Indian head, enhanced with the carved initials of fellow members. He was elected editor of the college's *Jack-O-Lantern* humor magazine for his junior and senior years, which came with a handsome annual salary of $1,600. At the time, Dartmouth tuition was about $250 a year. Norman befriended another student of modest means, Theodor "Ted" Geisel, who went on to create the enormously popular Dr. Seuss children's books. They were colleagues on the *Jack-O-Lantern* staff. Norman once caught Geisel, an inveterate sketcher, doodling in his hymnal during church services, and according to Geisel's biographers, Judith and Neil Morgan, Norman "lauded his talent if not his timing."

The Morgans picture Geisel and Maclean putting out the *Jack-O-Lantern* as pretty much a two-man show. Norman would hunch behind a typewriter and bang out a line or two and then invite Geisel to pick it up from there. "Sometimes he'd tell me what he'd written, sometimes not,"

Geisel recounts in the Morgans' *Dr. Seuss & Mr. Geisel: A Biography.* "But then he'd always say, 'The next line's yours.' And I'd always supply it. This may have made for rough reading, but it was great sport writing." Geisel was voted editor in May 1924, to replace the graduating Norman, and in later years he thanked his older friend for backing him for the job. "If Mac hadn't picked me as his successor my whole life at college would have been a failure." For his part, my father remembered Geisel as "the funniest man I ever knew."

Despite his numerous successes and friendships at the school, Norman never shook his outsider status and resented much about Eastern ways. He forever told a bitter story about his first night at Dartmouth, when he found himself sitting on his trunk in a cold, lonely dorm room amid unfamiliar surroundings. A group of upperclassmen came in and marked down a variety of assessments—a buck or two for the radiator, and so on. As the son of a provincial Presbyterian minister, he was both naive and nearly penniless. He paid up, but soon learned he'd been had—and found a way to get even.

"At the beginning of one year he and this other fellow dressed up as janitors, started at one end of the freshman dormitories, taking out radiators and fleecing the innocents," a student publication at the University of Chicago would report years later. "Their plan was simple but effective: they walked into the room of the fleeces, equipped with wrenches [and] prepared to take the radiator out. Just kneeling down, uncommunicative as hell, twice as natural as the typical janitor. The frosh would ask just what the idea was, receive no answer, repeat, and finally be met with the query, 'Have you paid your four-dollar radiator fee?'"

Paul began his college career in 1923 at the University of Montana. There simply wasn't enough money to send two sons to Dartmouth.

Once Norman graduated and began to teach at Dartmouth, Paul joined him, however, registering as a sophomore in September 1924 for his final college years. It was still a financial stretch, but the brothers did more than envy the rich college boys who brought girlfriends to Dartmouth for weekends: they found a ploy to lure one or two away. They had a cat that liked gin, and once they'd made the cat tipsy, they'd put it out to play. The cat's antics drew the attention of girls waiting for their dates, and things developed from there.

They wrote home with newsy items that often found their way into the *Missoulian*. In February 1925, they reported their escape from a fire in the rooming house where they were lodging. "The youths lost all their personal belongings, including a number of manuscripts which Norman was preparing for publication." Paul was active and successful at Dartmouth, joining the staffs of the *Jack-O'-Lantern*, the *Dartmouth*, and the *Tower*, and like Norman was a member of the Sphinx and Beta Theta Pi.

As might be expected, though, his literary career did not follow a smooth path. In a murky incident that was alluded to within the family with embarrassment and no details, Paul resigned from the *Tower* after a printer refused to run several stories on grounds they violated New Hampshire law about immoral material. In a letter to the *Dartmouth* titled "A Futile Struggle," Paul and his co-editor, William A. Hunt, declared themselves "heartily out of sympathy with the legal system that discriminates against the publication of material of undoubted literary value, while allowing the publication of frankly salacious material disguised as humor." He and Hunt said they thought it best for themselves and the school to resign, "tired as we are with the never ceasing struggle with smug hypocrisy."

By the end of the term in 1928, Paul was one math course shy of a Dartmouth degree and agreed with the school authorities to make up the deficit back in Montana that summer. He signed up at the University of Montana for Interim Algebra, not his strongest subject. The professor, Nels Johann Lennes, was a noted author with an international reputation. Lennes was also a political radical who, like Paul, hated the Anaconda Copper Mining Co. that dominated the political and economic life of the state. The two of them got on famously. Little was learned of algebra that summer, but much was said against the ACM. Paul received a solid grade of B and was awarded a Dartmouth College bachelor of arts degree, class of 1928.

He almost immediately landed a job with a newspaper in Helena, beginning a decade-long career in Montana journalism there and in Great Falls, covering everything from the police blotter to Rotary Club luncheons to the state legislature. Most notable was his coverage of the statehouse for the *Helena Independent Record* for legislative sessions in 1933, '35, and '37. Most of his coverage was straightforward journalism: tax legislation; the price of hunting and fishing licenses; votes on legalizing gambling. Montana politics, though, could be colorful. "In a wild, hectic night, when legislation was threatened with fisticuff, the house of representatives passed through the 50th legislative day, the last day for the transmission of bills to the senate, leaving 38 bills stranded on general orders and a number dead within committees," he wrote for the February 26, 1935, issue. An admiring gossip columnist once called Paul one of Helena's most eligible bachelors, remarking on his "shy and affectionate" nature. Norman often pointed out his brother's tender side. Paul never could bring himself to shoot a deer, for example, although he handled a shotgun with assurance; the boys could bring home a limit of grouse in those days just by stepping out the cabin door at Seeley Lake and walking the woods for an hour. Tough but tender, those Maclean boys, down through the generations.

DURING THOSE YEARS Paul built his reputation as a fisherman. He became adept at a technique called shadow casting, or casting a fly in continuous loops over likely water, skimming but not touching the surface, to create a shadow on the water in imitation of an insect hatch. This theoretically encourages a rise of trout, at which point the fisherman lets the fly land and reels in a catch. It's a difficult technique and of much-debated value in luring fish—there's more shadow from the line than the fly, for example, and fish find it easier to see what's on the water than what's in the air.

Jason Borger, a professional fly-fishing consultant, made shadow casts for the movie *A River Runs Through It*, standing in for Brad Pitt's "Paul." Shadow casting is a kind of ballet involving fisherman, rod, and line, and it's beautiful to watch, but there's no manual on how to do it. Borger and the film's fly-fishing production coordinator, John Dietsch, both experienced fishing guides, had to develop a technique for the movie. Borger had read *A River* just before his teen years, but had never before tried shadow casting "for fear of making the trout run, not rise." Borger and Dietsch determined, however, that the cast could be performed by starting with what's called a Galway cast, or two back-to-back forward casts, the first to the rear, the second to the front.

"The hardest part physically was the awkward back-handed move coming forward," Borger told me. "I ended up dressed as Paul for the scene's long shot. I should note that Brad Pitt, an athlete and physical quick study, worked out the movements and timing in short order for the scene's close-up. With some further fine-tuning, the shadow cast, at least the cinematic version of it, was ready to roll."

A quarter century later, when I contacted him, Borger passed along a tribute he'd written to shadow casting in the form of a Haiku:

Under a big sky
Shadows cast in a rhythm
Perfect memories

My father admired Paul for his skill but said that he'd never seen shadow casting fool a fish. But who's to say? Paul believed in it, he caught an awful lot of fish, and half of fishing is belief and persistence in what you're doing. Shadow casting does introduce one useful notion, that of presenting a fly in an unconventional manner. Paul's boyhood best friend, George Croonenberghs, master fly tier and fisherman, later developed a variation of shadow casting that was effective. He found that during the October caddis fly hatch, among the most important of the fishing year, skipping or skating an October caddis imitation across the water in the bumbling mothlike flight of the female caddis, who strike the water to deposit their eggs, can elicit a strike, especially if you quit skipping the fly and let it sit so the trout chasing it can catch up.

Paul fished harder, longer, and more imaginatively than other fishermen. He was nearly always the first on the water and the last to leave. He traveled light—a rod and reel, a hatband stuck with wet flies tied by Croonenberghs, a wicker fish basket, and a packet of Lucky Strikes in a shirt pocket. He waded deeper, faster water than others did, out where timid fishermen dare not go, and when the current swept him off his feet he laughed while he swam. With his powerful upper body, he could propel a cast out to the heaviest, impossible-to-wade water, the home of big rainbow trout. When the Blackfoot was dead water for fishing, which could happen then as now, he would go over to Cottonwood Creek, a gentle and meandering tributary, and wade in up to his chest, sinking deep into the stinky mud bottom. There, he'd catch a few—and later be banned from the family camping tent until he'd had a thorough rinsing. When a fishing partner was doing too well, Paul would throw rocks into his fishing hole. He could be reckless and he liked to gamble: he was lucky as a fisherman, but not as a poker player.

After work he'd drive out from town and fish streams like the Little Blackfoot near Helena. One time, right after he'd bought a new car, he was driving home in the dark after a fishing trip when his headlights picked up a rabbit bouncing along in the dirt road ahead. The rabbit, startled by the car, took off, and the race was on. The road followed section lines and made abrupt ninety-degree turns, which brought the race to a predictable conclusion. When Norman asked his brother a few days later how he'd managed to wreck his new car, Paul responded, "The rabbit made the turn and I didn't."

CHAPTER FOUR

THE RIVER OF THE ROAD TO THE BUFFALO

AS THE FAMILY scattered over the years the cabin at Seeley Lake became the common ground that brought us back together and secured the link to the Blackfoot River. Fishing the Blackfoot in the early twentieth century, when it all began for my family, was summed up in a headline in the *Missoulian* on August 12, 1928, "A million trout to every mile of Blackfoot river," which combines a Western brag with an element of truth. The Blackfoot held an abundance of trout but drew only a handful of fishermen.

The most acclaimed fisher of the river in those days was an eccentric song-and-dance man, rod builder, and fly tier who called himself Paul Bunyan and who on occasion hopped around Missoula on a pogo stick. He even used his adopted name, taken from the folk hero logger of the Upper

Midwest, on his driver's license and fishing licenses and put an image of the famed Babe the Blue Ox on a logo for his tackle company. Paul Bunyan, born as Norman Edward Lee Means in West Virginia in 1899, came to Missoula in 1921 to attend the University of Montana. His studies included aquatic and terrestrial insects of western Montana, which eventually led him to create his cork Bunyan Bug, much sought after to this day. The bugs started out as bass flies, big cumbersome things, but Bunyan discovered they also attracted large trout. He streamlined them and tied patterns to match different insects, the most famous of which was the salmon fly.

The *Missoulian* chronicled his many colorful activities, as dance instructor as well as fisherman. He'd entertained the troops in Europe in World War I as a song-and-dance man and carried on in performances and classes in Missoula. The newspaper dubbed him "the best booster the Blackfoot has," and reported that he didn't have to go far to catch a basketful. He'd take the streetcar to Bonner, get off near the mouth of the Blackfoot, where it joins the Clark Fork, and tie on a Bunyan Bug suited to the season, a salmon fly for June, or a mosquito for summer. "Then he starts fishing," the *Missoulian* recounted. "And he catches fish. This particular evening, he tied on a 'Paul Bunyan Round River Mosquito' fly, which he makes, and he landed

17 rainbow trout that weighed 16 pounds, dressed. This 'Paul Bunyan Round River Mosquito' is a weird looking fly. It is as big as a bumble bee, but it catches the fish." On that trip Bunyan tossed back about fifty fish that were twelve inches or under, following the "one-foot rule" for keepers.

Bunyan caught my father's eye. He purchased a couple of the bugs the first year they were offered in the 1920s, when they looked like cigar butts, and kept them in his fly box ever after. He also bought the later, more refined versions, fished them, and featured one in *A River Runs through It*, writing, "It was so big and flashy it was the first fly I saw when I opened my box." Bunyan designed but did not make the bugs he sold through his Paul Bunyan Fishing Tackle Company. "He made the Bunyan Bugs only if he had to during a hatch at the river," said his grandson Richard Rose, who grew up around him. "The women made them—my mother, aunt, and grandmother." Bunyan fashioned rods for himself, friends, and retail sale, often with wrappings the colors of a rainbow.

Bunyan was part of a group of early Missoula fly tiers celebrated for creating unusual, sturdy, and effective flies, a testament to not only their skills but also the rich nearby fishing waters. The elder statesman, Jack Boehme, often called the father of Montana fly tiers, gave public instruction in fly fishing and set a world's record in 1925 with a cast of one hundred twenty-four and a half feet. (Borger, the fishing stand-in for the movie of *A River,* said that distance or a foot or two more was the longest possible cast using the equipment of that day, and was not exceeded until the 1930s, when the double-haul technique was introduced and championship casts added another thirty feet.) Boehme owned a share in the Turf Bar on Main Street in downtown Missoula, which became kind of a clubhouse for the group, and ran a tackle business in one corner. His repertoire included shadow casting, as did Bunyan's, and Paul Maclean may well have picked up the technique from them.

Franz Pott, a Dutch wigmaker who'd immigrated from Germany, was a regular. He used his professional skills to weave individual badger hairs and other materials into thirty different fly patterns, a process he patented in 1934 that has been carried on to modern times. Watching and learning from this group of elders was a young George Croonenberghs, who became famous for his quill patterns, "the generals" described in *A River Runs through It.*

The gang from the Turf Bar showed off their catches, dozens of trout that on occasion weighed two or three pounds each, in a big horse watering trough in front of Bob Ward's sporting goods store. They filled the trough with ice and covered it with glass to keep the fish fresh.

The *Missoulian* cataloged one of Boehme's hauls in 1911: one fly, seven days of fishing, one hundred eighty pounds of trout. They were the pioneers of fly fishing on the rivers around Missoula, but they hardly were the first to discover the Blackfoot River.

FOR CENTURIES, NATIVE Americans wore a trail along the river as they traveled through the Blackfoot Valley and across the Continental Divide, out and back to the buffalo hunting grounds in the Missouri River country to the east. They called the Blackfoot River Cokahlarishkit (there are various spellings), "the river of the road to the buffalo." The trail—or rather, the road—along the river was a lifeline for tribes west of the Divide who followed it to the plains, in winter as well as summer, to hunt the buffalo that provided food, clothing, tools, and shelter.

Meriwether Lewis and a small party were the first white men to travel through the Blackfoot Valley and record their observations. Far from blazing new trail, they traveled the ancient road, so well worn that traces of it remain to this day. Lewis had separated from William Clark to broaden their explorations on the return journey of the Corps of Discovery in 1806. Lewis and nine of his men, five Nez Perce guides, seventeen horses, and his Newfoundland dog

Seaman parted from Clark at Traveler's Rest on Lolo Creek in the Bitterroot River valley on July 3, 1806, intending to rejoin Clark on the Missouri River.

The Lewis trip through the Blackfoot Valley has received little attention from historians. After crossing the Continental Divide, the party had a violent encounter on the Marias River with a small band of Blackfeet, and historians focus on that episode. The journey through the Blackfoot Valley was nonetheless a significant event. It marked the coming of the white man and the beginning of the end of the road to the buffalo, a visible marker for a way of life that had existed for centuries if not millennia. The name Blackfoot River began appearing just a few years after the Lewis journey. John Work, a chief trader for the Hudson Bay Company, led a brigade of trappers through the valley in 1831 and in his journal called it the Blackfoot River, as though that were the established name. (The name Big Blackfoot River appeared on a map as early as 1865, to differentiate it from the Little Blackfoot River to the south, but U.S. Geological Survey maps call it the Blackfoot River.)

Today, Highway 200 from Bonner at the confluence of the Blackfoot and Clark Fork rivers to the Continental Divide follows in a general way the ancient trail. Scattered signs remain of its presence in the form of short sections of deeply worn trail and lichen-covered rock cairns used to mark it. A few are well known, but some are recent discoveries that haven't yet entered the history books. Ron Cox, historian for the Seeley Lake Historical Society, has explored the road to the buffalo for decades on foot and by horseback and motor vehicle, and he and other local history buffs have made fresh finds. I found it intriguing not only that marks of the ancient trail exist, but that some are semi-secret or at least not common knowledge. I asked Cox, a friend and Forest Service retiree who calls himself a "dirt forester," if he would retrace the trail with me, and he generously shared what he and others have found. The journey of one hundred twenty miles from Traveler's Rest to the Continental Divide took Lewis four and a half days. Going back and forth over the route took me, sometimes with Cox, many more days, stopping, going back, moving on. The experience had the happy by-product of affording me a ground-level view of the Blackfoot Valley from stem to stern, or very nearly so.

AFTER PARTING FROM Clark at Traveler's Rest, the Lewis party crossed the Clark Fork and camped near a small tributary, Grant Creek, on the outskirts of present-day Missoula. They spent the next morning, July 4, at the campsite, sending out hunters and saying goodbye to the friendly

Nez Perce who had guided them over the mountains. The Nez Perce refused to accompany the party any farther, however, because they feared an attack by the Blackfeet. They warned Lewis he was heading into danger, but told him he would have no trouble finding the well-worn trail on his own. The party saddled up about noon and passed through today's Missoula. That part of the route can be followed in a general way by automobile, along the Mullan Road and then Broadway. The party forded Rattlesnake Creek at about the place Broadway now crosses the Rattlesnake, at a bridge that has a plaque from the 1930s mistakenly claiming it marks the July 3 campsite. They reached the confluence of the Blackfoot and Clark Fork rivers after riding ten miles from camp and turned up the Blackfoot, following the trail on the north side of the river.

Lewis recorded his first impression of the Blackfoot in his journal. He noted it was sixty yards across, turbid, and "wide deep and rapid. the banks bold not very high but never overflow." Neither the Clark Fork nor the Blackfoot appeared navigable to him, "in consequence of the rapids and shoals which obstruct their currents."

For the first upriver miles, the river flows in a narrow gap between steep mountains that in places on the south side, opposite the ancient trail, come down to the river and make foot or horse travel impossible. Highway 200 offers an almost continuous view of the river along this stretch, which has become one of the most popular for float fishing. Lewis described this leg of his journey as poor land, "timbered country, mountains high rock and but little bottoms." With few exceptions, the mountains are of sedimentary rock, part of the Precambrian Belt formation, and easily break off in crumbly sheets. The effect is dramatically apparent in these first miles. Layers of shale at various angles from horizontal to straight-up vertical rise above the river. The rocks, formed from sand and mud, were bulldozed into these shapes by a gigantic tectonic plate that geologists estimate moved east into Montana seventy to seventy-five million years ago. Freezing, melting, and other effects break up the rock, which sloughs into huge fanlike piles that can block easy passage along the river. The explorers noted occasional rough going, but never once complained they couldn't find the trail.

The party marched upriver for eight miles until the narrows opened into a flatland with grass for the horses, and they camped there. Today, the Angevine fishing access off Highway 200 is regarded as the likely place for this campsite. Cox thinks the party may have gone a short distance farther along to a spot that has freshwater springs, which would have been welcome with the Blackfoot running high and dirty. Artifacts uncovered there in recent times, he said, show it was an occasional Native American campsite; it's now in private hands. From the Angevine parking lot, it's only a short distance to the river, which runs hard against a wall of rock on the far, south side. The scene, masked from the highway by trees, appears much the way it did for the explorers. The day I walked over from the parking lot for a look, I startled a pair of Canada geese. They glided into the current and effortlessly rode it downstream. It was easy to imagine a campfire on the riverbank, and Lewis and his men lounging at their ease after supper. In his journal, Lewis said the evening was fine, the air pleasant—and no mosquitoes.

The next morning, July 5, the expedition got an early start, at six a.m. Lewis noted seeing an old Indian encampment of nearly a dozen lodges on the opposite shore: the likely site can be viewed today from Highway 200 milepost 10. A mile farther along, the highway crosses the river and proceeds through the Potomac Valley, leaving the river behind. Potomac Valley, where Native Americans dug for the bulbs of camas plants, today is used for field crops and pasture. The ancient trail stayed with the river and entered a narrow canyon that is part of today's Blackfoot Recreation Corridor, which offers twenty-six miles of public access. A gravel road follows the river through the corridor on the south side, opposite the ancient trail, until it crosses to the north side at Whittaker Bridge, about halfway through the canyon. From there, the road climbs the hills for easier going, just as the ancient trail did in places to avoid long river meanders, obstacles, and brushy river bottoms.

About eleven a.m. Lewis came out of the narrows into a "handsome and extensive Valley and plain," today's Nine-mile Prairie, a place of quiet beauty about nine miles long. It's three-quarters of a mile to several miles wide, bounded by the Blackfoot River to the south and a row of low hills on the north. Lewis noted that the trail passed at some distance to the left of the river, over by the hills. The Lewis party rode toward the hills, where a little drainage watered an aspen grove and created a green oasis. There they stopped to eat and let their horses feed.

Today the grove is easy to spot. The white mottled bark and quaking leaves of the aspen trees stand out amid the dun-colored prairie grass and the stately Ponderosa pine trees on the hills. This portion of the prairie is scrubby and relatively undisturbed; there are ranches and scattered homes farther north. I parked where the gravel road emerges from the narrows and walked on from there to the grove, about a mile away. Roughly halfway there I came upon two large, flattish, lichen-covered rock piles in rectangular shapes. Cox had told me about them, and their purpose is a mystery. Passing between them takes you straight to the grove, suggesting they could be Native cairns marking the ancient trail that Lewis followed, possibly worn to flatness by time.

After the stop at the grove, the Lewis party rode on for nine or ten miles until they passed what Lewis described as a "high insulated knob" and arrived at a clear, sparkling river not far above its confluence with the Blackfoot. They named it Werner's Creek in honor of William Werner, a member of the party. Lewis noted two swans in the creek. This is today's Clearwater River. Lewis's "high insulated knob" matches an abrupt and isolated hill immediately to the west of the Clearwater campground, just off Highway 200. If you park at the campground and walk a few hundred yards upstream you'll find that the high riverbank suddenly drops down to a low swale that's an obvious ford. Lewis's party may have crossed the Clearwater here, a little more than three miles upstream from where it joins the Blackfoot. Several miles straight east the Blackfoot enters a narrow gap that the ancient trail followed, just as did early wagon roads and now Highway 200.

The Lewis party did not venture up the Clearwater River and its chain of lakes. However, Sgt. Patrick Gass, a member of the party who also kept a journal, made the first written observation of that stretch of country. "When we had gone about nine miles we came to and crossed a river [the Clearwater], about 35 yards wide, which flows in with a rapid current from some snow topped mountains on the north, where the valley is two or three miles wide." Gass could not see to the narrow opening at the head of the valley, about two and a half miles away, where the Clearwater River emerges from Salmon Lake, the last big lake in the chain that includes Seeley. The Clearwater then rushes in an almost continuous rapid for about a mile in a narrow, steep gulch, what's now called Clearwater Gorge, before smoothing out in the broad valley below, the site of an ancient lake.

As the Lewis party moved on, past today's Clearwater Junction where Highway 200 meets Highway 83, Lewis noted that his view of the Blackfoot River to his right was blocked by a high prairie hill, a rounded heap of till left by glaciers that's easily seen from the highway. When the glaciers that filled the Swan and Clearwater drainages began to melt, they contributed their waters to Glacial Lake Missoula, which was among the largest ice dams known to history, about the size of Lake Ontario. The prairie around Clearwater Junction was at or near the lake's farthest extension into the Blackfoot Valley. Glacial Lake Missoula formed when ice dams blocked passes in the mountains to the west. When the dams repeatedly broke down during a warming period of about three thousand years, late in the last glacial age, they released titanic masses of ice and water that scoured the landscape, creating what are now the scablands of eastern Washington, and then ripped down the Columbia Gorge to the Pacific Ocean. In *A River Runs through It*, my father called it "the world's great flood."

Beyond Clearwater Junction, about three miles to the east, the Blackfoot flows through a narrows, but just before the pass the river briefly flattens out and can be forded in moderate water conditions. There's no mention in the expedition journals, however, of ever crossing the Blackfoot, which would have been a noteworthy and dangerous undertaking at high water.

The Lewis party went through the narrow pass, which today includes the popular Russell Gates campground and fishing access. The pass is known as Sperry's Grade for Charles Burton "CB" and Helen Sperry, who homesteaded there in 1899 and built a slab-sided roadhouse on the north side of the highway that's still there. The roadhouse was operated for many years as an overnight stage stop on the Missoula-to-Helena run. The Reverend Maclean was called to the Sperry roadhouse, according to my family's lore, to perform marriage ceremonies for several of the Sperry girls. "My father farmed and raised stock," one of the girls, Rachel, remembered for a local history, *Profile of Early Ovando 1878 to 1900*, by Hazel Jacobsen. She said he moved the family there from a ranch near Helena because he was "so taken" with the Blackfoot Valley's beauty and the abundance of grass and water. "There were miles and miles of open range," she recounted. "Everyone turned out their stock in the spring and rounded them up in the fall."

Coming out of the narrows, the Lewis party rode into an extensive prairie rendered uneven by many little hillocks or moraines, and sinkholes or kettles, the effects of the last glacier. The hillocks are mounds of debris stranded by a melting glacier; the sinkholes are places where the glacier left clumps of ice to melt. They camped that night near the mouth of a waterway they named Seaman's Creek for Lewis's Newfoundland dog. This is today's Monture Creek, later renamed for an early fur trader. Some have proposed changing the name of the creek back to the original, but local residents cite problems with property rights and other issues, and the name today remains Monture Creek. The Lewis party camped near the mouth of the creek and found evidence there of campfires about two months old, which they figured had been made by a war party on account of what appeared to be an attempt to conceal the fires.

Highway 200 crosses a bridge over Monture Creek about two and a half miles from its mouth, and a fishing access road for the creek branches off near the bridge. Nearby, Cox and others have located a previously unrecognized section of the ancient trail. It's on a sidehill, up from the access road. When Cox and I explored it together, we pushed our way through brush behind a utility building about halfway down the road and then went up the sidehill to find it. The trail is overgrown in spots, but it has a defined lip on the uphill side, as though worn from long use. It's too wide for a game trail, too narrow for a wagon, and just right for a horse or dog with a travois. Trees of long standing have grown in the track. The trail comes down from the prairie at a natural area, or close to one, to ford the creek. We walked the trail up to the prairie, but there it disappears.

Lewis and his party started out early the next morning, July 6, and splashed across Monture Creek, then rode on through open plains, noting the mounds and sinkholes. Lewis called the area around present-day Ovando the prairie of the knobs, and the name has stuck to this day. Here, they found more signs of a war party: fresh hoofprints. "We expect to meet with the Minnetares and are therefore much on our guard both day and night," Lewis wrote, using a tribal name loosely applied to the Blackfeet.

Their haste—plus the high, turgid water—explains why there is no record of them becoming the first white men to fish the Blackfoot River. The expedition started out with nearly three thousand assorted fishhooks—an astonishing number. The majority were used for trading purposes, for the metal hooks proved popular with the Indians, who made hooks of softer materials such as bone or antler. The expedition's premier angler, Pvt. Silas Goodrich, joined Lewis on this leg of the trip, and one is tempted to imagine Goodrich wishing he could fish the swollen Blackfoot. Although the word *trout* appears more than twenty times in the expedition journals, there is no mention of fish in the accounts of the Lewis trip through the Blackfoot Valley.

If Goodrich had wet a line in the Blackfoot, he would have angled for westslope cutthroat trout, which along with bull trout, arctic grayling, and whitefish were the native game fish in Montana's mountain waters. Rainbow and brown trout were introduced in Montana as early as 1889, following the railroad lines that spread across the state beginning in that decade. The rainbow flourished, interbreeding with but also severely reducing the range of the native cutthroat. Today rainbow trout are Montana's most sought-after game fish, but the state has stopped widespread stocking in rivers, though it continues in lakes and reservoirs. Instead, efforts are under way to bring back the cutthroat, the state fish, through protection, habitat restoration, and removal of non-native species. On the Blackfoot, it's not uncommon to hook a rainbow in the rough white water at the head of the hole, a cutbow hybrid in the middle of the hole, and a native cutthroat—or a close genetic relative—in the quiet water at the tail end.

AFTER CROSSING MONTURE CREEK on the morning of July 6, Lewis and his men continued on until they reached the North Fork of the Blackfoot, which they forded only with difficulty. Sergeant Gass wrote that the river was about forty yards wide, the current rapid, and the water up to mid-rib on their horses. A few miles beyond the North Fork, the ancient trail left the prairie behind and entered the Blackfoot Canyon, about fifteen miles long. The river has a different character in the canyon—it's a meandering stream that flows gently through flat brushy bottomland before turning into the heavy, rushing rapids and deeply etched holes that characterize it farther downstream. The ancient trail climbed into the hills in places to avoid the low marshes and brushy thickets, as Lewis described, noting how the party had passed over a steep bald-topped hill at the entrance to the canyon, which may have been Marcum Mountain.

There's another short section of ancient trail in the canyon, similar to the one at Monture Creek. It can be accessed from Highway 200, just east of milepost 65, but it's tricky to find. Cox and I drove past it a couple of times before he was sure of the place. We parked and hiked for several hundred yards, and then turned uphill and bushwhacked until we found what we were looking for. Like the section at Monture Creek, this one has an uphill lip, indicating long wear, is the right width for a travois but not a wagon, and has mature trees growing in it. We walked it for several hundred yards along a timbered sidehill until it gave out in a meadow, where the marks had been worn away by long exposure to the elements.

The Lewis party passed through the Blackfoot Canyon and out onto an expansive plain, where they camped on a small creek. Historians put this camp at Beaver Creek just west of today's town of Lincoln. The plain abounded in game, particularly beaver. The next morning, July 7, one of the explorers wounded a moose, which Lewis noted caused his dog Seaman much worry. The party then set out and soon arrived at Lander's Fork, beyond today's Lincoln, and followed it upstream, leaving the Blackfoot River behind for good.

There's a well-known section of the ancient trail, marked by a rock cairn, along the east side of Lander's Fork. It's near the Copper Creek Road, about three and a half miles from where it branches off Highway 200. When Cox and I visited the site, there was a pole fence built around the cairn to protect it, but the fence had fallen into disrepair.

The Lewis party crossed from Lander's Fork to the marshy Alice Creek drainage to the east, and from there went up to the Continental Divide. The spot most historians identify as their crossing place is today called Lewis and Clark Pass, though Clark never used it. Once they reached the top, Lewis looked east and recognized a landmark, Square Butte, which was familiar from the outward journey a year earlier. For the Lewis party, the way home was all downhill from there.

Lewis and Clark Pass today is accessible by a foot trail, a steady but not daunting climb of about 1.7 miles from the Alice Creek trailhead. The hiking trail is wide and well worn; it intersects at the top with the Continental Divide National Scenic Trail that runs from Canada to Mexico. A Forest Service sign marks the topmost site: "Lewis & Clark Pass. Capt. Meriwether Lewis, on his return journey, crossed the Continental Divide through this pass on July 7, 1806. Helena-Lewis and Clark National Forest." There's a rock pile at the crest suggestive of a cairn, but the stones are clean and without lichen, as though gathered in recent times. The day Cox and I hiked it, the surrounding landscape had a bleak and blackened look from the 2017 Alice Creek Fire, which scorched nearly thirty thousand acres on both sides of the divide.

From the top of the pass you can see far back into the

Blackfoot Valley, which despite the burn marks near the pass remains one of the most beautiful in Montana. As though waking from a dream of time past and finding it reflected in reality, there are places in the valley today, away from roads and ranches, where you can stand, look in all directions, and see a landscape much as it appeared centuries ago. The river of the road to the buffalo has etched itself into enduring shapes at the foot of granite mountains. The ancient road itself has left evocative traces, though these are few and far between. The last glacier left behind telltale dips and moraines that even the colossal floods of Glacial Lake Missoula could not wash away. It's a land with a long-term memory.

CHAPTER FIVE

"THEY WERE BEAUTIFUL IN LIFE"

MONTANA WAS STILL a frontier when the Reverend Maclean brought his family to Missoula just over a century after the Lewis trip, but his pastorate at the First Presbyterian Church, from 1909 to 1925, played out against a backdrop of notable national and international events that affected him, his family, and the state. After the Big Burn of 1910, with the Reverend as the Old Testament patriarch who stood firm to reassure a trembling flock, World War I, and the 1918–19 Spanish flu pandemic by turns required the Reverend to display compassion and courage and challenged him, in the words of the psalmist, to find still waters to restore his soul. The Blackfoot River is not still water, but there's a spirit-quieting stillness that lingers in and around it.

America entered World War I late, two and a half years after it began, but it took a heavy toll nonetheless. The First Presbyterian Church encouraged youth in many ways, and the Reverend Maclean was always on the lookout for young men to take leadership roles. He spotted a likely candidate in Paul Logan Dornblaser, a parishioner and student at the State University of Montana (later the University of Montana) who played left tackle and captained the football team, and invited him to teach Sunday school and take charge of the church-sponsored Boy Scout Troop 2. Dornblaser declined, arguing that his other responsibilities took all his time and effort. "I know your son Paul very well," he wrote to Mrs. T. F. Dornblaser on July 10, 1912, explaining the situation, "and like everybody else who knows him here I respect him highly . . . He is 'straight goods.'" Within the next five years, Dornblaser completed a law degree, became a deputy county attorney, and was elected a trustee of the First Presbyterian Church and vice president of the University of Montana Alumni Association. On June 20, 1917, less than three months after Congress voted to enter the war, in April, Dornblaser enlisted as a private in the Marine Corps despite urging from his father, a Civil War veteran, to wait and see if the war ended quickly, as many hoped and expected it would.

On September 12, 1918, after promotion to corporal,

Paul Dornblaser saw his first day of action in France, less than two months before the war ended. "Went out into No mans land and over the top this morning," Dornblaser wrote in a diary. "A terrific barrage! Wonderful to me! Tanks, trenches and advancing lines—wonderful!" The wonder didn't last. By October, Dornblaser was making repeated trips over the top under heavy fire in the ultimately successful battle that month to take Blanc Mont Ridge in western France, which had been a German stronghold since 1914.

"Oct. 6th Sunday. Our losses were heavy this morning," he wrote. "The machine gun ahead opened up and gave us hell. This sure is some no bon [good] sector. A boy on my left has just relieved himself and was hit with two machine guns through his trousers. They can see us better than we can see them. We are now standing by. . . . Some Hell! Heavy shelling, seemingly from all directions." Accounts of his wounding two days later, on October 8, vary considerably, but the most reliable version, from the captain of his company, states that Dornblaser, after "going over the top" twice that day without injury, volunteered to show relieving troops where to take up position and was machine gunned. He died of his wounds about twenty-four hours later. "The doctor and the nurse each wrote me a letter, telling me how bravely my son bore his sufferings, and assuring me that all was possible was done to ease his dying hours," his father, T. F. Dornblaser, later wrote in an autobiography.

In 1919, the Reverend Maclean participated in a tribute to Dornblaser, helping plant a memorial tree for him on the Missoula County courthouse lawn. The Reverend saw it as an opportunity to speak for nature, as he often did, as well as for a friend, a fallen soldier, and a valued church member.

"A tree is the biggest living thing in all the world, it lives longer than any living thing," he said, in an echo of his natural science training at Pictou Academy. "This tree that you are planting today, if it prospers, will be young when you are old, and will be flourishing in life, when we and our children and our children's children are returned to dust, and are no more remembered in this land of the living. He was a 'great boy,' and took his boyish spirit with him into manhood's estate and up into the place of battle where brave men laid down their lives in that bloody struggle of which History will forever speak with awe." Today, the tree is gone, but there's a World War I memorial in front of the courthouse with a statue of a doughboy and the names of Missoula's war dead.

By the time he delivered the soldier's tribute, the Reverend Maclean was no stranger to sudden death, even for an experienced minister. On the same day as the last entry in Dornblaser's diary, October 6, 1918, the enlisted men in training at Fort Missoula enjoyed a Sunday off, mingling with the city's civilian population. Many soldiers reported ill that evening after returning to the fort. The next day, Monday, the *Missoulian* recorded that the Spanish flu had infected the post and twenty-five men had been "quarantined for examination." The disease traveled quickly in wartime, with troops moving easily by train and concentrated in places like Fort Missoula. Montana lost a recorded 4,187 people, about 1 percent of its population, to the flu. In an echo of the Covid-19 pandemic a century later, the main tools to combat the disease were quarantine, good hygiene such as handwashing, disinfectants, and limiting public gatherings. Church services in Missoula were curtailed and ministers, barred from their pulpits, were obliged to speak to their flocks in essays published in the *Missoulian*. Saloonkeepers, though, kept their doors open until near the end of the pandemic.

Under the banner "Your Pastor Speaks to You Here," the Reverend Maclean published a sermon in the newspaper three weeks after the flu was first reported in the city. He called on his flock to show "faith that casts out fear and all its torments" to meet the crisis. "The times through which we are now passing call for that kind of faith," he said, "a faith that makes us strong and of good courage and hope and cheer." The First Presbyterian Church suspended services for seven Sundays, and no church members were lost to the virus. Attendance lagged even after the quarantine was lifted, and financial collections suffered. "We were obliged to postpone painting and repairing the Manse [the pastor's home] for the lack of funds," the church records report.

In time the Macleans resumed normal activities, which included camping along the Bitterroot and Blackfoot rivers in summer when church duties lightened and they could get away for a trip. They could always return to Missoula for Sunday services.

The Bitterroot and Blackfoot rivers are in opposite directions from Missoula, but each is accessible from parallel roads and both run into the Clark Fork River near town. The Clark Fork is bigger water and has larger fish, but it was heavily polluted in those days from mining and smelting operations at its headwaters near Butte; where it passed through Missoula it was an open sewer. Clark Fork fish tasted unhealthy. The Macleans favored the Bitterroot and the Blackfoot rivers, which were both clean and loaded with fish. Once the cabin at Seeley Lake was completed in the mid-1920s, the Blackfoot became the family's river of destination.

The boys, Norman and Paul, spent much time with

their parents at the cabin, where they slept on the screened porch. Norman was sleeping there alone one morning when he was awakened at dawn's first light by the sound of a great fluttering in the distance. As he became fully conscious he realized the noise came from a massive flock of ducks, stopping over during their migration. He slipped out of bed, found his clothes and a shotgun, and quietly stole down to a marshy pond along the lakeshore to the south where the ducks had settled. He told me the sky blackened when the ducks arose; all he had to do was raise the shotgun and pull the trigger to bring dinner home.

As the years passed, the boys went off to school and took summer jobs, which limited their time at the cabin. My father told a story about how he and Paul decided to hike all the way back to Missoula at the end of a weekend, leaving in the dark in time to make it to town to start work at nine a.m. They would follow trails over the Jocko Pass, into the Rattlesnake drainage, and down from there to town. Their father drove them several miles from the cabin to a jump-off spot. The road trip is about fifty-five miles, but foot and horse trails could be more direct. Even so, it was a daunting undertaking. My dad and I once went looking for the jump-off place, and we found a general location but no trailhead. He was never clear, either to me and perhaps to himself, whether they had done it just the once or several times—and exactly how they had done it. Over time, though, the hike achieved near-mythic status in the family and beyond. In recent years, Seeley Lake community leaders tried to identify the route and make it a memorial trail, but they, like my father and me before them, couldn't come up with a credible candidate.

In *A River Runs through It,* Norman describes in detail what happened when he, Paul, and their father fished together for the last time. The scene was near where Belmont Creek empties into the Blackfoot. Today, the wooden pilings of the old railroad bridge across the creek are still there, close to the river, but the road is higher up in the hills. My father and George Croonenberghs once tried to find the exact place of that scene, where Norman and his father sat together on the bank and watched Paul work magic on the river for the last time. Norman and George couldn't fix the exact place, except it had to be near the mouth of the Belmont. Some things are better left in mystery.

WITH THE BOYS away so much, Seeley Lake came to belong more and more just to the Reverend and Clara Maclean. He mounted a one-and-a-half-horsepower Evinrude "Elto" outboard motor on the stern of his rowboat, lit a pipe, and went trolling for trout with a string of spoon-shaped brass lure "flashers" separated by cherry-colored glass beads to imitate a school of fish. He used a copper wire line to get the contraption down to the fish and wrapped the other end of the line around a slab of wood with handles. We used those "cowbells," as we called them, until my father banned them as unsportsmanlike. In the fall, the Reverend took a green, canvas-covered duckboat he'd built up to the head of the lake. He'd pull it into the reeds, put a Remington twelve-gauge shotgun across his lap, and read the Bible in Greek while waiting for a flight of mallard or canvasback ducks to come scudding in. He and Clara often stayed at the cabin into November, when they would drag a bed in front of the open fireplace and feed the fire during the night.

But it was cold, mightily so. "I don't know how they stood it," my father told me. They'd go to the bridge over the Clearwater River at the outlet of the lake and drop handlines with big hooks baited with chunks of beef off the bridge, angling for brown and bull trout making annual spawning runs up the river.

It wasn't all solitude and ice. The Reverend had a formidable public presence, but at the same time he was accessible to a generation of young sporting men in Missoula, and to them he was a cherished figure. One youngster, Davey Roberts, from a prominent family of parishioners at First Presbyterian, remembered him as "companionable" and tolerant with the young blades. On a fishing trip to the Blackfoot late in the year with a group of young fellows, as Roberts remembered, the Reverend slipped and fell into the water, getting a thorough soaking. Hypothermia threatened. The young men helped him to a nearby ranch house where the rancher offered him a glass of whisky to warm him up. The Reverend, a teetotaler, was known for the phrase "The ruin of Scots men is Scotch whisky!" But on this occasion, he did not refuse the glass. When Roberts asked him how he liked it, my grandfather replied in a Scottish burr the whisky had revived, "*Verrry* warming!" Roberts went on to a distinguished career as an outdoor writer, and in a column about the Reverend described how he began each year at the cabin, soon after the snow went out.

It was at this time each year that Old Maclean went to his cabin on Seeley Lake. He worked around a good deal, clearing out dead limbs that the snow and ice had brought down, fetching in wood for the cookstove, sweeping here and raking there. But most of all, in the spring, Old Maclean liked to fish the lake for trout. It was, in the later seasons, about the only fishing he could do with comfort and success, for the years were heavy on his shoulders.

He was long in the mountains. He had come at

the turn of the century from the tight little hills of Nova Scotia, where he'd preached in the Presbyterian pulpit, to the same church in Western Montana. At first, he told me afterward, the tremendous masses of the Rockies were unfriendly, cold, after the smaller wooded hills of home. But that was only for a while.

As he grew older he took on the character of the mountains which he came to love. He was quiet, like the giant peaks about him; quiet and dependable; calm, full of philosophy and goodness, humor and common sense. He was my father's best friend. Afterwards he became my friend and fishing companion. In the last few years he referred to himself often as "Old Maclean," and it stirred a smile always when we younger anglers took it up.

When the Reverend left the pulpit in Missoula in 1925, he took the post of secretary for the Synod of Montana for the Presbyterian Church in Montana and Wyoming; they moved to Helena, where he continued to preach on occasion and regularly headed back to the cabin at Seeley Lake. He had a reputation as an eloquent speaker, but his diction and cadences had an English flavor, as well they might have had: he read the King James Bible and his favorite writers were the English religious poets, Gerard Manley Hopkins,

George Herbert, and William Wordsworth, the latter a double favorite who combined religious conservatism with a love of nature.

My grandfather worked hard at being American, as first-generation immigrants often do, and in his later years achieved a voice more straightforward but still elevated. One text surviving from that period shows him at the height of his literary and spiritual gifts. The occasion was a tragic event that drew him back to Missoula three years after he left.

On a cold and foggy Saturday afternoon on the last day of the year, December 31, 1927, A. J. and Maud Gibson, an architect and his photographer wife, set out in their car, perhaps to do a little shopping for the upcoming New Year holiday. They came to a railroad crossing just outside the city limits and began to drive across the tracks. The train engineer saw the car, set his brakes, and sounded his emergency whistle. Afterward, he said the driver apparently did not see or hear the train and kept going. The engine struck the car full-on. Perhaps the Gibsons could not see through the fog; perhaps they could not hear because they had the windows up for the cold. My father said the couple, in their mid-sixties, were hard of hearing, and that, too, may have contributed to the accident. A coroner's jury exonerated the train crew from any blame.

The Gibsons were among the Macleans' oldest and best friends. They had greeted the Macleans when the family first arrived in Missoula and had taken them straight to their home. They had camped, socialized, and prayed together. The Reverend Maclean returned from Helena to speak at their funeral service at the First Presbyterian Church—the church that was his project and Gibson's design—on January 4 of the New Year. The new pastor, the Rev. D. E. Jackson, conducted the well-attended funeral service, and Reverend Maclean offered a tribute. It was short, like much of the best of American writing, but he put into it a lifetime of faith, hope, love, and learning, and as was his custom he made liberal and repeated use of the word *beautiful*. He employed for effect one of the oldest of literary devices—anaphora, the repetition of the first part of a sentence.

"We are here to share the sorrow and the gospel of this hour," he began.

"I am reminded of a couplet—'They were beautiful in life and in death they were not divided.' They were beautiful in their love for each other, a love that grew in tenderness and sweetness and made their lives increasingly beautiful. Without children of their own, their love intensified and made them precious to each other.

131

Those who saw them in the intimacy of their home life understood the affection that they had for each other.

"They were beautiful in their love for other people. Children in this city will carry the everlasting remembrance of these two. They were beautiful in their charity and love for the less fortunate in circumstances. They gave without show, and did many kindly deeds which will make them long remembered and blessed by many families here. They were beautiful in their love for their friends. They were friendly and had a host of friends, to whom their home was always open.

"The things he did showed that he had the soul of an artist, and the things she did showed that she had the soul of a poet. They may claim this church as their monument—behind their zeal and affection was a rare love for Christ. We speak of the sadness of this hour with our hearts burdened with the tragedy of it. I'm not so sure that we should do that. They were enjoying a sweet hour of companionship when the crash came, and then, hand in hand, they went home to heaven."

CHAPTER SIX

"PAUL! PAUL!"

THE YEAR 1928 promised to be a pivotal one for Norman and Paul, both now finished with college. For Norman, there were two questions. Should he seek permanent employment with the Forest Service or teach high school in Montana? And what to do for a wife? He found the second question the easiest to answer. In one of his "Lovely Jess" letters from the ranger station in Gold Creek, he told her about a potential literary success. He'd had a request to use two of his poems—"kid verses," he called them—in a new edition of a popular anthology of children's verse. He wasn't getting his hopes too high, but it could be a plum if it worked out.

Working for the Forest Service left little time or energy for writing, but he was glad of the days in the mountains because it helped clear his mind. "I'm just feeling for the typewriter now," he wrote. "It's somewhere in the darkness." Poetry seemed like a distant world, "so far away now, clear out of my range of thinking. That's just the way I want it to be for the time—I'll come back to it fresh." But he wasn't glad about being away from Jessie. "This time next year—if we get only the even breaks—Jess—next year at this time—we shan't be so far apart. We shall be together, tied by bonds 'that no man can put asunder.' Hush, Jess. How I love you."

Jessie had a promising job by 1928, as an assistant to the state auditor in Helena, after two years as a history major at the university in Missoula. She had a good head for numbers, a gift from her storekeeper father, whom she remembered marking down prices in pencil on a scrap of butcher paper as a customer put together a big order. He'd nimbly total it up in his head. Once married, it was Jessie who kept the accounts and wrote the checks, but there were limits. When Norman gave up typing after they married, she did not fall into the trap of becoming his secretary. He switched to writing almost everything, books included, in a cramped longhand that generations of typists at the university and elsewhere prided themselves on learning to decipher.

Norman's career found its footing that year. After being turned down for a high school teaching job in Missoula, he made the decision to leave for the University of Chicago, starting there at the bottom of the academic ladder while also working on his doctorate, a prerequisite for a professorship. The lot of a teaching assistant, he discovered, could be a dismal one. One of his duties was grading freshman English papers, reams and reams of them. He described the routine as "going home late Friday afternoon, having a couple shots of Prohibition gin, going to bed right after dinner, and reading thirty 1000-word compositions on subjects as irrelevant as 'How to Fill a Silo,'" which he joked, sourly, had made him an expert on corn.

In the classroom, he acquired a reputation for making difficult authors such as Rabelais and Chaucer come to life. "Norman F. Maclean is one of the best liked guys around this place," one student remembered. "He is best remembered because when we were freshmen we used to go to class only when he lectured. His classes are always overrun." Students sometimes "slept out" to register for his courses, spending the night in sleeping bags to be near the head of the line and secure a place.

Another of his students, Marie Borroff, who went on to a distinguished career as a poet and became the first woman English professor at Yale University, remembered the first time she heard him lecture, not in a classroom but before a general audience in the U of C's cavernous Mandel

Hall. By then, Borroff remembered, he had become a figure at the school not only for his teaching but because he
hailed from a "wilderness outpost," was good with a rifle,
played a rough-tough game of handball, and was an expert
on Gen. George Armstrong Custer—as well as Aristotle.
Those characteristics plus his "raw, reluctant" speaking
style brought his listeners to attention and made what he
said stand in high relief. He paused for a full beat before
he spoke, she recalled: he did not rush as a lecturer, a
fisherman—or an author. "When he did begin to speak,
it was in that extraordinary—always recognizable, always
inimitable—manner; that raw, reluctant utterance that
somehow contrived to lend color to whatever he said." In
a turnabout from teacher to student, my father said that in
later years he regularly submitted his prose to Borroff and
had "published practically nothing that has not profited
from the criticisms." She urged him, he noted, "not to con-
centrate so much on the story that I would fail to express a
little love I have of the earth as it goes by."

Leaving Montana physically never meant moving away
in spirit. In those early years, he wrote poems and story
notes on thin, unlined paper that he kept in a binder. His
themes were mostly about the West: one yellowing page
has a single handwritten sentence, "He was a good mule
skinner."

A more serious effort, "The Lumberjack," clearly fore-shadows the plot of one of the stories in *A River*, "Logging and Pimping and 'Your Pal, Jim,'" which depends on the tension between the Norman character and a tough logger. The form is poetic, the writing hammered prose:

THE LUMBERJACK

For a day or so there hadn't been anything between us
But the sound of the saw.
He was sore at something—
Sore at himself, I guess,
Though I didn't know for sure. He was sore so much
    of the time
That I couldn't be bothered. I'd just shut up on the
    talk,
That's all.
I had to anyway, to keep my end of the saw going.
When he got sore he worked harder than a Swede.
So we were bucking up a log
When, all of a sudden
In the middle of the cut,
He straightened up and said,
"Let's pull the plug."
I asked, "Why?"

He said, "We've worked here two weeks already.
I'm beginning to feel like an old head
On the job."
I said, "All right, let's go."
So we threw the saw and axe into the brush
And went.

It took him a dozen years to complete his doctorate. When in 1940 he finally marched up the aisle of Rockefeller Memorial Chapel, amid the pageantry of the annual Convocation ceremony, the university's president, Robert Maynard Hutchins, held the diploma back as Norman approached. While hundreds in their academic regalia looked on, Hutchins passed a few light remarks to Norman about how he'd wondered if this happy day would ever arrive, before handing over the document. Two years later, Hutchins asked him to serve as dean of students after the incumbent resigned to enlist in the military following America's entry into World War II. My father had applied to join naval intelligence and been offered a commission, but he turned it down to take the dean's post, which he held from 1942 to 1945. When that job came to a close Hutchins offered him a choice of what he wanted to do next, thinking he'd surely ask to stay in administration. Being dean had given my father an ulcer, however; he said he'd hated most having to kick kids out of school for academic failure. He asked simply to return to the English department. He knew he'd made the right move, he told me later, when his stomach settled down enough that he "could switch from scotch and milk back to bourbon and ditch." Traces of an intestinal ailment, though, followed him the rest of his days.

Once back teaching English, he did not hesitate to introduce his students, urbanites to the core, to the joys of fishing and an outdoor life. The U of C, after all, promoted cross-disciplinary studies. When Jean and I were in our early teens, he once invited us to a class he was teaching on the story of a big fish, Ernest Hemingway's *The Old Man and the Sea*. He asked the students at one point about the technical problem Hemingway faced in trying to tell a book-length story with only one human figure, the Cuban fisherman Santiago, who hooks a giant marlin. Who besides Santiago could play the role of a main character and provide the conflict necessary to move the story along? he asked.

I thought it was the easiest question I'd ever heard in a classroom, but it stunned the students into silence. After a pause of embarrassing length, I raised my hand, and my father called on me. "The fish!" I said.

My dad took a beat, smiled a beatific smile, and said, "That's my son!"

———

MY UNCLE PAUL, too, found his vocation in 1928. After he completed Dartmouth's requirements for graduation that summer, he spent the fall looking for a job. He and Jessie became close friends and he wrote to her as "Dear Jakie" or "Jake," using her tomboy nicknames, and even addressed letters to "Miss Jake Burns," though after she and Norman married, Paul switched to "Dear Jess." In October he wrote Norman that he and Jess had attended a football game together in Helena and afterward a performance at the Marlow Theatre of *The Trial of Mary Dugan*, a melodrama about a showgirl accused of killing her millionaire lover. "Jess had bought loge seats!" Paul exclaimed. "The play was darn good," he wrote, "about as good as you would see anywhere."

His job search was well under way, and he'd answered an advertisement for a job opening that Norman had sent him with a formal application, edited by their father. "I answered it as I saw fit," he wrote. "It is hard work saying good of oneself. I joked about my accomplishments . . . but Dad cut off all the fringes." He told his brother, "Don't worry about getting me a job," and said he was even willing to go east to find one. "If there isn't anything doing I will get to Boston some way. I don't want to loaf too long. I did turn down a job here—selling perfume and hot water bottles.

As soon as I can get in touch with a cattle train I am going east . . . job or no. I hate to leave the west but I will be back."

Within months, Paul landed the first of a series of newspaper jobs, starting in Helena and soon thereafter in Great Falls, for both that city's *Tribune* and its rival the *Leader*, and then back to Helena. Being a cub reporter can be as humbling as being a teaching assistant, as Paul discovered. In a letter to Jessie, he recounted how his assignments at the *Tribune* amounted to a round of civic lunches with an unvarying diet of baked ham, boiled potatoes, and cabbage salad. "Monday is Kiwanis day," he told her, and he included the unchanging menu. "Tuesday, it is the Lion's club, hale fellows, jolly bunch of happy and prosperous not to mention splendiferous bastardbusinessbums, preparing for their regular luncheon meeting. Once again I sit down to baked ham, boiled potatoes, and cabbage salad. And then comes Wednesday . . . 'tis Rotary day."

Same lunch, same routine, slightly different venue all the way to the week's end. He tried to keep a light tone while recounting his money troubles, but his creditors apparently did not share the good humor. "I am being pursued. I lose weight. My eyes have the hunted appearance, I cower and shy at a piece of paper lying on the street. I wear gloves for fear of leaving finger prints. I owe money." His life, for sure, wasn't funny.

"I haven't a job," he wrote Norman at one point, complaining about his lowly position at the paper. "I just fool around. I often think of crawling around the floor and getting dirty so they will know I was doing something." The *Tribune* was stingy with bylines, and one of the few mentions of Paul's name in the paper during his tenure there is not about him but about his brother Norman. "Norman F. Maclean will arrive Monday from Chicago where he is assistant professor of English at the University of Chicago," the *Tribune* reported on August 3, 1930. "He returned recently from a tour of Europe, and while here will visit his brother, Paul Maclean. From Great Falls, he will go to Helena to visit his parents, the Rev. and Mrs. J. N. Maclean."

Even fishing could be a disappointment. "You could hardly get to the banks of the rivers," he wrote Jessie about a May trip to the cabin. "It rained eleven times on the way over but I had the vague idea we were getting away from the rain. When we reached Seeley it was sort of headquarters for the rain. The clouds seemed to assemble over the cabin and whoever was in charge of them tried each one out every few moments."

Despite the seeming uselessness of trying, Paul made the effort. "I used everything but gunnysacks and old tires to no avail. I think if I saw a fish during my time out I would have jumped in and endeavored to save it from drowning. I have never seen such high water." He always had Montana, though, and always he, Norman, and Jessie had each other. "All the time I wonder how your life goes, if there are good times and easy hearts," he wrote to them. "I hope to see you both soon, we must not forget each other ever, we make a kind of a three peopled universe."

Paul and the *Tribune* eventually parted ways. "Things in Great Falls finally got so tough they let their last star reporter go out into the world without visible means of support," he wrote Jessie. "I felt I wasn't having the broad general experience that I should be having; writing up nothing but suicides, you understand. Only the high price of gun shells is keeping down the mortality rate." He took the separation in stride, regarding it as a vacation. He'd been over to Wolf Creek and discovered in this next to last year of the Prohibition era that Ken Burns "was making his own beer and had a cache in the basement of the dance hall—and he had the only key." Paul joined the queue for the dance hall "although there was no dance," he wrote, and followed a "deep worn path to the basement door."

Paul eventually got his big chance in journalism. He was hired by the *Helena Independent-Record*, which assigned him the key beat of statehouse reporter beginning with the 1933 legislative session; his byline soon became a familiar one on the newspaper's front page. Paul's coverage was

respected, but it also could be two-fisted. His own newspaper carried downright admiring accounts of two fights he
got into in 1936 as a reporter. The first involved a mysterious
episode of political chicanery at the state capitol. The incident began when Leonard Young, state railroad and public
services commissioner, discovered a dictaphone hidden in
his office on January 19 of that year. Wires led to the adjoining office of another member of the commission, Jerry
O'Connell. Paul and other reporters heard about the find
and showed up about one a.m. The press was denied access
to O'Connell's office, and so was Young. Paul, quoted in
the newspaper the next day, said that when he tried to put a
key in the office lock, three railroad commission clerks as-
saulted him and "a fistfight ensued." The governor, Elmer
Holt, showed up, too, but no key could be found to fit the
lock. The governor and others broke a window between
the two offices and crawled through to Young's office to
discover the dictaphone with missing parts—and an open
window. The assumption was that during the scuffle and
confusion in the hallway, someone had sneaked through
the exterior window and retrieved them. "I have made no
definite plans for pressing an investigation," the governor
said. Clearly, a political spy operation had been uncovered
and Paul had tried to get answers. He also wound up with
parts of the dictaphone, which upon receipt of a written order from the governor he handed over to a state custodian.

In November, he got into a fistfight with W. O. Whipps, secretary of the recently deposed state highway commission, who had objected to an article Paul had written. The fight started after Whipps, by Paul's account, called him "a series of names which commenced with 'contemptible rat' and became more pointed as they continued." The *Helena-Independent* account remarked that Paul "stood the verbal attack until well known 'fightin' words' were mentioned." Paul's philosophy of fighting was straightforward. If it looked like a fight was about to start, be sure you landed the first punch. Bystanders often stop fights after the first blow, and if you are the one who delivered it, you win. Likewise, if the fight continues, you've started one punch ahead. Paul reported that Whipps told him, "I took a beating but I got my money's worth." Not reported in the paper, but known elsewhere, Paul had a reputation in those years for going out with a friend looking for trouble, and if they failed to find some, they would fight each other instead.

After covering the 1937 legislative session in Helena, Paul left Montana and followed his brother to Chicago, telling friends he hoped to come back to Montana if things worked out for him there the way he hoped. The move, though, was part of a full-press effort by his family to settle him down and give him a future with more promise. He embarked for the big city on March 12 of that year with the high ambition of becoming a columnist for one of Chicago's many dailies. The plan was for him and Norman to return to Montana each summer, gradually take over the cabin as their parents aged, and never lose the link to Montana and fishing.

FOLLOWING HIS BROTHER, Paul tried to find a job on a Chicago newspaper, but the town's institutions were running then, and to this day, mostly on clout, a Chicago word that combines power, influence, and patronage. As Chicago mayor Richard J. Daley once remarked about his hiring practices, "We don't want nobody nobody sent." Paul didn't know anyone who had clout with the newspapers, and his résumé as an itinerant Montana journalist failed to make up for it. He took a job arranged by his brother as an assistant in the University of Chicago's department of publicity and press relations. The family story is that the head of the department, George Morgenstern, a friend of Norman's, tried to get Paul a job with the City News Bureau of Chicago. City Press, the bureau's informal name, was a cooperative that gathered news for the city's dailies and acted as a boot camp for journalists, a role it continued to play throughout the twentieth century. Morgenstern was new to his post, however, and hadn't yet worked his way into the city's power structure.

By the time I came along more than three decades later, Morgenstern had pocketed enough favors to make a call to City Press, and I had my first press pass within days. City Press honored clout, but it also offered a side entrance into the news business for those who had never taken a journalism course and had no experience, and it did this for me, my wife Frances, my son John Fitzroy—all onetime City Press kids—and for many others until sadly it succumbed to financial pressures at the close of the century. It was a colorful place that lived by the motto "If your mother tells you she loves you, check it out." By the time I joined City Press, an overzealous administrator had cleared out old applications such as Paul's and that of a suburban Oak Park resident who'd also been rejected, or so it was said: Ernest Hemingway.

Paul began his brief career for the U of C writing press releases and organizing conferences and seminars. In a letter home, he told his parents they would be proud of his role in arranging a conference on texts of the Old Testament. When Paul joined Norman and Jessie at the university, they made a stirring trio. They hailed from wild and woolly Montana, mythologized by no less a literary figure than F. Scott Fitzgerald in his 1922 novella *The Diamond as Big as the Ritz,* a story about a preppy on the East Coast whose father was "the richest man in the world" because his Montana mansion was built over a diamond one cubic mile in size. The brothers were good-looking, athletic tough guys, and Jessie was a Scots-Irish beauty whose open personality was rare for a woman with her looks—and for a faculty wife. In time it would be said of her, "She was the only one who'd talk to the young faculty wives."

She and Paul had an instinctive mutual understanding as freer spirits—freer, anyway, than Norman, who seemed born to responsibility, and born to be his brother's keeper. A University of Chicago student and friend, Gene C. Davis, remembered the brothers as close and alike, but not in all ways. Paul was "more volatile than Norman," he said, and "Norman more pensive and poetic." Paul made a name for himself at the university as a handball player, "champion quality" by the school's standard, Davis said. "Everybody liked him."

Paul became an instantly recognized figure by young women at the school. He was in his early thirties, fit, and movie-star handsome. Secretaries timed their lunches so they could be in the Quadrangle when Paul Maclean walked its pathways. He took rooms close to his brother and sister-in-law, had dinner with them as often as not, and reestablished their "three peopled universe." There were exceptions, though, to his dutiful behavior. Davis said Paul could be found some mornings in a favorite chair at a fra-

A postcard circa 1915 of the upper Blackfoot River.

The author fishing the upper Blackfoot about a century later.
Photo by Alec Underwood

The Maclean boys, Norman and Paul, on a family camping trip
on the Bitterroot River in the early 1910s.
Photo by Maud Gibson

Paul Maclean fishing the upper Blackfoot River.
Photo by Norman Maclean

A school photo of
Paul Maclean.

Norman, Clara, and the Rev. John N. Maclean
in Missoula with family dogs, late 1930s.

The Reverend Maclean on Seeley Lake, 1930s.
Photo by Norman Maclean

Seeley Lake.

The Mann Gulch Fire, August 1949. *USFS*

John Henry Burns (left), proprietor, in the Arthur and Burns General Store, Wolf Creek, with clerk, 1912.

Postcard of Wolf Creek, Montana, circa 1940.

George C. Croonenberghs, master fisherman,
June 14, 1918–September 22, 2005.

A box of flies tied by George Croonenberghs for the author, 1995.

The author and Croonenberghs geared up for a hike into
Morrell Lake to camp and fish, 1950s.

Norman Maclean takes his children, Jean and John,
with him fishing the Blackfoot River, 1947.

The author on the
porch of the cabin
at Seeley Lake with
a largemouth bass,
1947.

Jean and John Maclean at the Montana border crossing sign on a cross-country trip from Chicago to Montana, 1950s.

LEFT AND BELOW: The author fishing with his uncle, Ken Burns, for grayling and trout at a high mountain lake in the 1960s. Note the sinking raft. *Photos by Norman Maclean.*

Typewriter used by Bert Sullivan, Seeley Lake postmistress, to type the original manuscript of *A River Runs through It.*

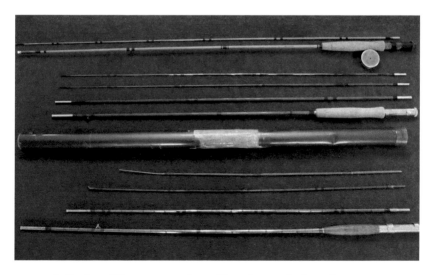

A display of three generations of bamboo rods: from bottom to top, the Reverend Maclean's H. L. Leonard, Norman Maclean's Granger Champion, and the author's custom-built rod.

The author fishing the upper Blackfoot River in the fall.
Photo by Alec Underwood

"A fish of great size and power":
Blackfoot River rainbow with the salmon-like head.
Photo by Jay Proops

The lower Blackfoot River in late fall.

The author's son, John Fitzroy Maclean, fishing the upper
Blackfoot River in the evening.

ternity house sleeping off a rough night. And he acquired debts.

ON THE LAST full day of Paul Maclean's life, Sunday, May 1, 1938, he had about $50 in his wallet, having cashed a two-week paycheck. He took his girlfriend, Lois Nash, twenty-nine, a redheaded Irish nurse, to an afternoon White Sox game at Comiskey Park at Thirty-Fifth and Shields. She later said she and Paul had been dating for two months and were engaged to be married, which came as news to his brother and sister-in-law. The White Sox played the St. Louis Browns, who won by a score of 7 to 5.

Paul made a day of it and took Lois for a leisurely dinner at Hyde Park's best restaurant, Morton's at Fifty-Fifth Street and Lake Park Avenue. After dinner they visited friends, and Paul then delivered Lois back to her place at 5143 Kenwood Avenue. He left about ten-fifteen p.m., saying he was headed home. Paul walked south across the Midway toward his lodgings at the Weldon Arms Hotel, 6235 Ingleside Avenue, just a couple of blocks from where Norman and Jessie lived, at 6020 Drexel Avenue. But he did not go home.

The following events occurred within a few blocks of one another just south of the university, in the Woodlawn neighborhood near where Paul lived. Not long after mid-night, on Monday, May 2, Sidney Sorenson saw a man behaving strangely across the street from his home in the 6200 block of Eberhart Avenue. The man threw himself to the ground and then arose, pretended to stagger, and walked a short distance away to the corner of Sixty-Third Street and Eberhart Avenue. Sorenson said "two colored women and a Negro man" apparently became alarmed and moved off as the man approached. He last saw the man, whom he later identified as Paul, at one-fifteen a.m.—it's not clear how an identification was made. Another witness, A. D. Adkinson, who lived nearby on East Sixty-Fifth Place, said he saw a young man scuffling with two others at Sixty-Third Street and Drexel Avenue that night. The man, whom Adkinson identified as Paul, walked away from the scuffle and the others drove off in a car.

Then shortly before five a.m., Edward Miller was awak-ened by loud talking in the alley behind his home at 6234 Rhodes Avenue. He got up and looked out into the yard but saw no one and went back to bed. When the noise per-sisted, he got dressed, went out to investigate, and found a man lying unconscious in the alley. Miller didn't have a phone in his home and had some trouble finding one to call the police. When he did, the address he gave was garbled. It was not until six-eighteen a.m. that the Chicago Police received another call of a man down in the alley behind Sixty-Second Street and Eberhart Avenue. They found Paul alive but unconscious where two alleyways join in a tee. Police found his wallet nearby, empty, and three $1 bills and a dollar in change in his pockets. Police also found in one of his pockets a matchbook for the Vogue Liquor House, a bar near where he lived. He was transported to Wood-lawn Hospital, where nursing staff at first thought he was passed out drunk. When they turned him over, however, they discovered a deep wound in the back of his head indicating that he had been severely beaten or struck with a heavy object. He died in the hospital at one-twenty p.m. without regaining consciousness.

Those are the bare facts from police and coroner reports and from the account in the *Chicago Tribune*, which my father said covered the story accurately and with restraint. The murder was a sensation, though; the alley where Paul was found was near Sixty-Third Street and Cottage Grove Avenue, known as "sin corner." It was said that every vice known to man was for sale there, and not every newspaper handled the story with the same care as the *Tribune* did. The *New York Post*, for example, reported that prostitutes had been active in the vicinity that night, but the police investigation found no link between them and Paul, and such activity in that neighborhood was hardly a rarity.

My father speculated that Paul had gone wandering through the neighborhood that night, as he had done as a reporter back in Montana, simply to acquaint himself with his surroundings. "He liked to walk around in odd sections of the city," Norman told a coroner's inquest. "He was a newspaper reporter by trade, and he was from a small town. He liked to walk around, just to see the town, Saturday afternoons and sometimes at night. I had warned him that this was not Montana, and he couldn't walk around with impunity looking at the sights, but he didn't seem very particularly persuaded by my argument." Jessie thought it possible Paul had gone looking for trouble, as he sometimes had in Montana, and then found that Chicago didn't play by Montana rules. She often wondered if he had been given just a few more years and a lot more luck, whether he might not have turned a corner, married, started a family of his own, held a steady job, and found supportive friends. Paul would've had to give up a lot, though, for that kind of life.

An investigating officer, Detective Sgt. Ignatius Sheehan, became interested in the story of the feigned stagger, and knowing that the university sometimes sent in private reports on vice in the district, he surmised that Paul may have been conducting an investigation for the school. University authorities denied this, as did my father and Paul's boss, George Morgenstern, who dismissed the theory as utter nonsense. Another theory was that Paul's gambling caught up with him and he was attacked for bad debts. But this scenario, which was carried through in the movie version of the tale, is quite unlikely for late on a Sunday night, in a heavily African American neighborhood, supposing that debt enforcers were sent to collect or encourage repayment. After several weeks of investigation, Deputy Coroner C. J. McGarigle asked the police officer who oversaw the inquiry, Capt. Mark Boyle, for his conclusion.

"Did the police come to an opinion as to how this occurrence happened, whether it was robbery or otherwise?" McGarigle asked.

"I am of the opinion that it was a robbery," Boyle replied. And that's the way it remains on the police books to this day: a robbery gone bad, a murder unsolved.

NORMAN ALONE ACCOMPANIED his brother's body back on the long, overnight train journey to Montana. When he once tried to tell me what that trip had been like, he couldn't find words. After the funeral in Missoula, he spent several weeks of compassionate leave with his parents at the cabin at Seeley Lake, and he was able to describe this experience years later.

"It was early May, and the forest floor of the cathedral of thousand-year-old tamaracks was covered with dogtooth violets, which are really lilies. Around the lake they are often called glacier lilies, probably because it is only about twenty miles from our lake to the glaciers. We thought they were the most beautiful and fragile flowers we would ever see, and we tried not to walk on any of them. My father aged rapidly. He never hunted ducks again and had to give up most of his trout fishing. His feet dragged when he walked, as if his leg muscles had atrophied so he could not fish the big river anymore and even the creeks that were hard to get to. Mostly he fished in the lake in front of our cabin in a flat-bottomed boat he had made many years before."

If Paul's story had ended there it would have remained a shocking family tragedy best left in the past. It did not. The portrait Norman managed to create in *A River Runs through It* gave Paul a lasting afterlife as the charming rebel, doomed but beautiful and gifted with a fly rod. He was forever the younger brother who struggled for an independent life and went down fighting. Norman's vision of him, though, brought the consolation of shared experience, taken to an eloquent level, to a host of brothers and sisters who have reached out to wayward siblings only to see them twist and dodge away as Paul did.

Many years later my father would come down from the cabin to the lake in the evening when the world had turned to gentleness, and I would sit on the bank watching for a fish to rise. Without acknowledging my presence but knowing I was there he would call out, "Paul! Paul!" his face nearly incandescent with the light of remembrance and expectation.

CHAPTER SEVEN

A FEEL
FOR GREATNESS

THE QUEST FOR literary recognition can take strange forms. In our summer isolation at the cabin we had a radio in a cabinet the size of a dresser rigged to copper antenna wires strung around the ceiling; it first ran on batteries, but thanks to rural electrification we eventually had power. On clear nights when radio waves could bounce off the ionosphere without interference, we could pick up broadcasts from Salt Lake City by the Utah Symphony orchestra, bringing Mozart to the wilderness, but that was about it.

The limited reception hit my father hard one summer. He came in one day from picking up the mail beaming goodwill and announcing that a question about fishing he'd submitted to a radio sports show had been read over the air—and he'd been awarded a bundle of prizes! An initial notice telling him only to "Be sure to listen . . . tell your friends to listen" had been sent to Chicago and forwarded from there to Montana, only to arrive long after the broadcast. The subsequent letter he held in hand explained that his question had been read on the air, he'd been credited by name, and the prizes included a "fine hand-made Granger fly rod from the Wright & McGill Company of Denver, Colorado."

The rod, made of bamboo, was so fine he'd never have bought it for himself. In those days, we'd wear worn-out work boots, shirts, and pants for fishing and we'd have a single rod apiece, either a brittle bamboo or a heavy fiberglass one that was about as nimble as a telephone pole. His joy at the prize, though, was accompanied by a sense of frustration. "They read my letter and they used my question and I didn't hear it!" He promptly wrote the radio station director and asked for a transcript of the show, and miraculously one was mailed back to him without delay.

"We are sorry, indeed, that you missed the Fishing and Hunting Club of the Air on July 19, in which the answer to your question was broadcast," the radio director replied. "We are enclosing herewith that portion of the script which dealt with your suggestion." His question was, what should a fisherman do when a big fish rises to his fly but misses it? "Mr. McLean [sic] writes: When the average fisherman gets a rise from a really big trout he's apt to cast right back into the same spot with the same fly," the transcript read. "Is this advisable, or should the fisherman change to a different size and different color fly and rest the fish a while before casting again?"

Experts on the show disagreed on which technique is preferable, except to say "a lot depends on the mood of the fish." One remarked, "Did you ever notice how many thumbs you had on each hand when you try to change a fly in a hurry after a big fish rises?" I'd seen my father in that situation try both methods at different times, and a lot does depend on the mood of the fish. A trout actively feeding on a hatch is likely to take the fly if it's cast right back, figuring he'd simply missed another helping. A fish that comes up just for the fisherman's one fly probably has seen enough, especially if it's a large fish, and won't rise a second time even for a different fly. These aren't rules, though, and the fish gets the biggest say.

The prizes soon arrived in a huge package that was opened with great anticipation. The items that emerged included "a complete set of more than 100 artificial lures and fishing accessories," which were mostly large feathery things with treble hooks and cowbells meant for trolling, or perhaps for window displays. These were handed to my sister and me as toys. Never mind the barbs, we were a fisherman's kids and already savvy about hooks. Some of those things are around the cabin to this day on their original cardboard display cards. There was a canister of Kentucky Club smoking tobacco and a pipe from the show's sponsor; they were set aside for my pipe-smoking Uncle Ken. And finally, there was the nine-foot, three-piece Granger Champion bamboo rod in a crimson metal case with a well-machined screw top. It took about one heartbeat for the rod to become my father's favorite. He fished it all his life, mostly reserving it as a second rod for dry flies in the evening. Once in a while he would hand it to me on the river and say, "Here, try this one for a while," probably to give me the feel of greatness.

I remembered that remark years later, after I'd inherited the Granger rod along with the rest of my father's fishing gear. Checking up on the rod's pedigree, I discovered the Champion wasn't the top grade of the Granger line, but to this day it's regarded as a fine bamboo rod. I stored it away in a basement locker awaiting the time—say, a quiet evening on the Blackfoot—when once again it could summon up the feel of greatness. And then I forgot about it.

At some point, the locker flooded and water got into the metal case. By the time I discovered what had happened, the bamboo had turned black and soft, almost mushy, on the bottom third of the three rod pieces. The movie of

A River Runs Through It had just come out, and Orvis, the sporting goods company, had provided rods and other gear for the production. Orvis had a rod shop that I'd dealt with before, when I'd sent in an Orvis rod that I'd broken: the company has a twenty-five-year "fix it or replace it" guarantee for their own rods and they'd replaced that rod with no questions asked. This time, I sent in the Granger rod with a note explaining what had happened. I didn't ask for special favors, but I hoped and expected they would do whatever could be done. When a representative called to say the rod was fixed and ready, I asked the obvious questions: How much did I owe? Was the rod in good enough shape to be fished again? They weren't charging for this job, the rep said. But I'd be wise not to try to fish the rod. When it came back, you could see a slight discoloration on the damaged sections, but Orvis had refinished the rod from tip to butt, and to use the family word, it was beautiful.

LIFE IN A LOG CABIN with no indoor plumbing except for the line from the lake to the kitchen sink, no telephone, and no heat except an open fireplace may seem barren and difficult. But the place was well suited for human warmth and contact, notably on Sunday nights, when neighbors gathered there for dinner before heading home for another workweek. The main room of the cabin would heat almost to stifling from the open fire and press of bodies. After dinner, to which everyone contributed a dish, we settled down for the evening's entertainment, Western-style storytelling around a campfire. This meant an uninterrupted narrative by a single speaker to whom everyone paid attention. No cross talk. My father acted as storymaster, giving the floor to one person and then another, encouraging them to draw out their tales. Humble stories of hunting and fishing or visits to relatives gained stature played against a backdrop of Montana's wild landscape. We heard of terrible winter blizzards in which you had to string a rope as a guide from the house to the outhouse. "If your hand lost the line, they wouldn't find your body until spring." And of miners around Wolf Creek who soaked for hours in their first bath after winter let up, to loosen their long johns enough to take them off. "They'd worn them all winter and their hair had grown through the wool."

In those years, my father was searching for his own story, a narrative based in Montana that would fulfill his ambition to be a creator as well as a teacher of literature. In the summer of 1949, a year after he won that bamboo rod, he went alone to the cabin for a few weeks, leaving us to swelter in Chicago. I don't remember the rationale, but I do recall my mother being more than a little put out. On

August 5 of that year a fire blew up in a narrow gulch along the Missouri River a few miles southeast of Wolf Creek, my mother's town. Her brother Ken, a volunteer firefighter, and other local men were called out to fight it. The blowup on the Mann Gulch Fire overran and nearly wiped out a smokejumper crew dispatched from Missoula after it was first spotted, an event that commanded headlines across the nation. While the ashes were still hot, my father left the cabin and drove over to Wolf Creek, where he and Ken borrowed a vehicle rugged enough to get to the fire ground, located in the Gates of the Mountains Wild Area, now the Gates of the Mountains Wilderness. In the ashes of tragedy my father had found his Montana story, or one of them, but it would take decades before he started to put it down in words. He waited so long that despite working on it for more than a dozen years once he started, he came up just short of finishing the tale and seeing it to publication. When you consider his excitement at his brief moment of radio fame, you can imagine what this cost him.

THE CABIN TOOK WORK to maintain, from sweeping the larch needles off the roof each year to the ritual of firing up the stove several times a day to boil water for dishwashing—and when Jean and I were small, to wash diapers. Fishing was a break from chores, but you can't fish all the time, and if a social event loomed it often took on outsize importance. News of a visit by a living legend created no small stir for us, back in the 1950s. When we learned that Elers Koch, who had fought the Big Burn of 1910, was making a pilgrimage of old age to his family's lakeside cabin, located next to ours on the side opposite the Croonenberghs, the event took on the aura of a historic occasion. In many ways, the Koch family and mine had grown up together with the Forest Service. Both families lived in Missoula and in the 1920s built the neighboring summer cabins at Seeley Lake. The families mingled and became friends.

"Each summer started with a two-day sixty-mile horseback ride from Missoula to our cabin, and ended the day after Labor Day in the autumn with a similar return trip," Koch's son Peter wrote in an introduction to his father's autobiography, *Forty Years a Forester*, which he guided to publication years later. "Dr. Maclean taught me, at age ten, to tie flies, and in the 1930s we spent many pleasant days together pursuing trout in the streams and rivers in the vicinity—despite the fifty-eight-year difference in our ages."

A native Montanan, Koch had graduated from the Yale Forest School to become one of Pinchot's Young Men or "Little GPs," rangers of the U.S. Forest Service under its first chief, Gifford Pinchot, a founder of the school. Koch advanced to the position of assistant regional forester and chief of timber management in the Region 1 Northern Rockies headquarters of the Forest Service in Missoula. He was a man of slight build but remarkable physical abilities, a fine horseman and extraordinary hiker, said to knock off ten miles after dinner on occasion to make an even twenty for the day. He was also a thinker and writer. He had bravely published an article a quarter century after the 1910 big burn advocating a let-burn policy for wildfire, at a time when Forest Service higher-ups favored—and then institutionalized—a policy of full suppression of all fires. Observing the result of the vast efforts to control fire, he had asked a question that retains its relevance to this day: "Has all this effort and expenditure of millions of dollars added anything to human good? Is it possible that it was all a ghastly mistake like plowing up the good buffalo grass sod of the dry prairies?" He had retired in 1944 and now in the 1950s was making what proved to be his last visit to a place he had loved long and well.

The cabin sites, leased from the Forest Service, lie beneath an extraordinary stand of western larch trees, sometimes called tamaracks. Koch, who had studied the larch trees, had counted nine hundred fifteen growth rings on one fallen giant, aging it at nearly a millennium. "In the wide glacial valley on the west side of Seeley Lake, in the Lolo National Forest of Montana, is the finest stand of western larch in the Northwest—in the world, one might say," Koch wrote in *American Forests* magazine in 1945. "Fortunately preserved from logging operations, which removed the timber from adjacent lands over thirty years ago, this tract of several hundred acres is as unique and as beautiful in its own way as the better-known redwoods or the sugar pines of the Sierra."

Who or what act of man had saved our larch had always been something of a mystery. My father theorized that the stand was a geologic island, protected by water and mountains, taking his cue from Koch. "The great age of this stand of larch is probably due to its fortunate protection from fire by natural barriers, the lake on the east, and on the west a wet meadow and the wide Clearwater River," Koch wrote. That was the best theory of the day, but it could not have been more wrong. It was not at all the absence of fire that had preserved the larch, it was indeed the regular recurrence of fire.

Studies in modern times have shown that Northern Plains tribes regularly ignited low-intensity fires to spur regeneration of grasses. The tribes would camp at Seeley Lake in summertime, bringing their fire-management practices with them. "Until late in the nineteenth century, fires burned through Seeley Lake's larch forest about four times per century, much more frequently than in other larch-dominated forests," Stephen F. Arno wrote in "The Seeley Lake Larch: Living Link to Indian and Frontier History," a 2010 article in *Forest History Today*. Arno, a retired research forester for the Forest Service, intensively studied a portion of the stand that had never been logged. He concluded that Native Americans had likely set most of those fires, which occurred every twenty to thirty years. The regular fires cleared away brush and saplings and allowed the remaining larch, which protect themselves from fire with thick bark and by dropping their lower limbs as they grow, to reach enormous size.

Ron Cox, the historian for the Seeley Lake Historical Society, also researched the matter and determined that the Forest Service had played a major role in saving the stand of larch. Cox credits Ambrose Norton, Forest Service Lumberman (an actual title of the day), for inspiring this when he was in charge of a massive 1906–11 timber sale on the east side of Seeley Lake. The sale comprised fifty million board feet of timber, the largest sale ever made by the Forest Service up to that time. Norton, with a flair for romantic and flowery language, ordered the preservation of a "belt of trees" along what is now Highway 83 to preserve the "wildness and beauty . . . whispering its story to the winds of the Rockies as it solemnly awaits the coming of other generations." Norton's "belt of trees" got him in trouble with his superiors, Cox noted, just as the let-burn article later did with Koch, and for this and other reasons Norton was transferred to Wyoming. His successor in charge of the timber sale was Jim Girard, a timber cruiser who had been employed only a few years earlier to do repair work at a mill owned by the Big Blackfoot Milling company, which had applied for the timber sale. A conflict of interest loomed.

Girard, who had no formal education and hailed from a large, poor family in Tennessee, would one day be known as the patron saint of timber measurement. He worked for logging companies, scaling logs and working in mills, until 1908 when the Forest Service hired him to help with their huge timber sale. Girard realized he'd have to educate himself if he wanted to advance and he took correspondence courses in English, trigonometry, algebra, and cost accounting. He also spent many Sundays and evenings being tutored by a physician, a Dr. Randall, who owned a summer cabin at Seeley Lake. Girard also became good friends with Norton, the local ranger. He learned his lessons well and had a fine eye for observation. When timber company executives complained that he consistently scaled too high, to their disadvantage, Pinchot sent an inspector to Seeley Lake to check his work. The inspector verified the measurements and recommended that Girard be put in charge of the entire timber sale, and Girard replaced Norton in that responsibility.

In a letter to Pinchot, Girard described his friend Norton as a "gentleman and scholar" who was "intensely concerned with the interests of the Forest Service but was unfamiliar with western conditions or the lumberman's problems." Norton's many proposals to protect trees, Girard wrote, would have "broken any company with limited resources." Girard took a judicious approach, approving the sale on the east side of the lake, but sparing the stand on the west side, the one Koch wrote about and that Arno later studied.

Girard had a receptive audience in Pinchot, an ardent outdoorsman who had become familiar with Seeley's larch groves before being named chief of the Forest Service. In the summer of 1896, Pinchot had hiked with a companion through the Swan and Clearwater river drainages, in what he later called the best trip of his life. He made the trip at his own expense to see firsthand the region's vast Forest Reserves, which Congress had authorized there and nationwide five years earlier. The two lived off the land while scouting the country, much of which was later declared national forest, a decision influenced in no small part by Pinchot's observations during that trip. "To me it was a fairy land, in spite of the mosquitoes, which were so bad that I wore gloves, a flour sack over my shoulders, and a handkerchief over my ears and neck," Pinchot wrote in his autobiography *Breaking New Ground*. The giant larch trees proved especially memorable. "Huge western larch, my favorite among all American trees, and Western Yellow Pines and Douglas-firs made us good company," he wrote. "Green above but blackened at the base, they told the story of great forest fires. I was seeing this forest in about as intimate a way as it was possible to see it. In these glorious surroundings new facts in Forestry called for notice and explanation at almost every mile."

After encountering grizzly and black bears, a dangerously swollen Swan River, and one lonely trapper, Pinchot and his companion crossed the divide into the Clearwater drainage. "We halted for a short night on the bank of a most beautiful lake," he wrote in an unpublished manuscript. "Tired as we were, the impression it made upon us both, with its forest-clad shores, the distance, and just the faintest ripple on its surface, was keenly delightful."

What helped clinch the future of the larch, too, was the dedication in 1953 of a sixty-acre grove of the trees near our cabin, including the thousand-year-old behemoth, rated the largest in North America. That grove is named for Girard, a memorial to the man who helped spare it. My father and I happened to drive by the grove the day a Forest Service crew was installing a memorial plaque mounted on a boulder and we stopped to chat with them. Today, the town of Seeley Lake holds a popular Tamarack Festival in October, when the larch needles turn golden before they shed, the only conifer to do this.

Pinchot, Koch, and my father had in common both the Forest Service and high-powered educations in the East—Pinchot and Koch at Yale University, my father at Dartmouth—and they worked hard throughout their lives to bring together those two worlds, the life of the mind and the outdoors. Koch's impending visit to his cabin at Seeley Lake had special significance for my father, who had long admired Koch, a reverence that touched on envy. His yearning for the kind of life Koch had lived so successfully as a writer as well as a man of forests and mountains gnawed at my dad with animal intensity, and would continue to do so until he found his own way to bring those worlds together. As the day for Koch's visit drew near, he now spent hours prepping his family on how important it was, as an event in itself and as a chance to ask questions about the men, policies, and forests that Koch had known.

When the great day arrived, we were asked to stay away until evening to give Koch time to rest and be with his family. At the appointed hour my father led us along the path under the towering larch trees, through huckleberry bushes and patches of kinnikinnick, for the gathering at the Koch cabin. Koch, who in his younger days had ridden horseback between Seeley Lake and Missoula, now had to be helped out onto the cabin porch and settled into a chair. We gathered round, the young like me finding spots on the floor at his feet. Shadows were gathering. In the dim light we looked up at a small man of great age whose main feature was a pair of startlingly large eyes set deeply into the nearly translucent skin of his face. He said something in a muffled voice and hovering women scurried to take an old, dusty buffalo robe down from the wall and wrap it around him. His face twisted into a grin. With his body enveloped by the robe the eyes seemed even more prominent, and they scanned us like beams from a lighthouse.

We settled down and my father took out his notebook with its questions. I do not remember what he asked, but Koch responded with long silences and very few words. My father grew frustrated, speaking more loudly, more insistently. Eventually those prominent eyes dimmed and shifted downward, and something muffled was said. The brief interview had come to an end, leaving my father feeling empty. The Koch aura has stuck with me, however, as an image of a tribal elder with a mystical connection to the land we all loved, Seeley Lake and its larch. Koch did not live to see the vindication of his brave stance for healthy fire in his earlier years. Not long after this visit, after suffering terribly from arthritis, he was found lifeless in his home in Missoula with a pistol near his hand.

WHEN I WAS in my late teens, my father and I spent several summers on our own at the cabin, working around the place in the morning and fishing in the afternoon and into the evening. We counted up at one point and discovered we'd fished thirty-one days in a row. There was no catch-and-release ethic in those days, and we soon filled the cabin's freezer with milk cartons that had big fishtails sticking out the top. Our idea of conservation was to catch-and-give-away to the nonfisher folk in the town of Seeley Lake, who appreciated the protein. In the mornings we did chores like cleaning up the kitchen and cutting firewood. We used a two-man crosscut saw, the proverbial "misery whip," to buck up fallen trees. After long practice, we'd learned to keep a constant rhythm and make the saw spit sawdust and sing metallic music at the same time. Then we'd turn to other matters. He'd prepare for his fall classes by reading Words-worth or Shakespeare for two hours, no more, no less. He didn't want to be disturbed during that time, and I was free to roam or read as I pleased, just as years before he had been released by his father after homeschooling.

My freedom meant wandering the lakefront, perhaps

talking to my one hundred imaginary brothers, and catching the occasional largemouth bass. I invented names for the brothers, created to help fill my need for companionship, an unseen brother being a familiar pattern. I'd get lost in a daydream of all of us living together like early mountain men, leaving civilization behind to hunt and fish for our daily sustenance, a conflicted dream of solitude amid company. My abundant free time also meant deep immersion in a volume of Sherlock Holmes stories that I found by chance on a cabin bookshelf, which helped point me toward a lifetime career as an observer.

In the afternoons, my dad and I would pack up our fishing gear and head for a river, not always the Blackfoot. The Swan River was a favorite alternative. The pavement on Highway 83 ended at that time at the divide between the Clearwater and Swan drainages, and the gravel road from there up to Kalispell kept the travel light. We had the Swan mostly to ourselves. It's a pretty river, but it warms in summer and the fish head downstream to the cooler depths of Swan Lake to the north. Nonetheless, there are deep pockets in the Swan that hold fish, and as the weather cools toward fall the migrants return, especially spawning brown trout.

By the time we quit fishing we were chilled from wet-wading and the evening drop in temperature and ready for a mug of hot tea laced with bourbon whiskey. I'd heard the tea-and-whiskey drink was popular among the rugged outdoorsmen of New Zealand. We tried it and experienced an instant reviving effect, especially when it was laced with sugar. The trick is to keep the liquids separate until it's time for a drink so the tea stays hot and the alcohol doesn't evaporate. The mixture became a favorite with us, and my father introduced it to others so regularly that it became known as "a Maclean."

After we'd hiked back to the car, we'd take out a thermos of tea and a pint Mason jar of whiskey. We often parked by a bridge where we could stand sipping a hot "Maclean" from our mugs and watch the river sparkle with the last rays of light from a darkening sky. As the level of liquid in the Mason jar declined, warmth arose in our bodies and our eyes brightened. My father then would recite one of his dad's favorite sayings in a rhythmic church voice, as though speaking from a lectern. "As my father told me, it's not the miles you drive all day that are the most dangerous; it's the few you drive after you've been drinking!" And then he'd hand me the keys to the car as though it were a great gift. I was feeling no pain by then and took the keys in that same spirit.

We had a fun game on the way back along Highway 83, which follows a twisting path through heavy forest parallel to the Clearwater River. The trees came right down to the highway and in the dusk large numbers of deer would slip from the surrounding trees to cross the road, bolting at the approach of a car, or they'd stop still on the roadway and stand there wide-eyed, fixed in the headlights of an oncoming vehicle. Our game was to drive fast enough to get a thrill from the deer but carefully enough to avoid killing one and wrecking the car. We tried to make it back to Seeley Lake before ten p.m., when the last of the few places you could buy a meal there were closed for the night. If we were late, as often happened, it was a sandwich at the cabin and then bed, in my case sometimes in the same clothes I'd worn fishing. (For the record, I never killed a deer and never wrecked a car—and close doesn't count.)

The Swan was a fine fishing stream on its own merits, but it wasn't the Blackfoot River. In those days we often fished the Blackfoot without seeing another fisherman, especially in the evening on weekdays when the locals needed to be home. My father and I mostly fished apart, as was the family custom, but we kept a connection by gathering anecdotes for later telling and by keeping a tally of fish caught and lost. It was more a serenely hypnotic experience than a lonely one.

One evening we were fishing a giant horseshoe bend along Ninemile Prairie, opposite the aspen grove where Meriwether Lewis and his party had stopped to dine, and we soon lost sight of each other. When the last rays of reflected light failed on the water, long after the land had turned dark, we struggled to find each other along the high banks that edge much of this stretch. The brush along the bank rustled in front of me and my father popped out, his face a picture of such high excitement it cut through the dark.

"What's happened?" I asked in alarm. Maybe a big fish? No, something else.

"I ran into a bear!" my father said. "Or we ran into each other."

He had been scrambling through the willows along the bank and met a bear scrambling through the brush in the opposite direction. They were both taken by surprise, and my dad went one way and the bear the other.

"He's still down there somewhere, I didn't see him come out," my dad said. "I think it was a black bear." That was a relief: this was grizzly bear country, although the griz mostly stayed high in the mountains. The most dangerous moment with a bear—the abrupt and unexpected meeting—had passed safely, but there was still a startled black bear rambling about close by. Now we were torn between getting the hell out of there and trying to get another look at the bear, and curiosity won.

We went hunting the bear, walking the high bank and peering down into the brush, hoping at least to see the willows sway to mark the hidden path of the bear below them. It's astonishing how a creature as enormous as a bear can simply disappear into the wild right in front of your eyes. We searched without success until it got so utterly dark that the shapes of the mountains, the river, the banks, and the prairie all blurred together under the stars, and we turned away and headed for home.

Of all those times my dad and I fished together until we ran out of daylight, the most enduring picture that I've kept of my father is of coming upon him one evening at sunset on the Blackfoot River, when the fish were rising and our attention should have been on the water. Instead, he had put down his rod and was staring skyward. A crimson sunset spread across the whole of the Blackfoot Valley, the kind of incendiary spectacle that second-rate artists try and always fail to put on canvas and that Charlie Russell comes closest to capturing in his paintings. My father by then had escaped the bonds of the Reverend's Victorian Christianity, but the heavens still had a pull on him. He stood there next to the river, framed by the bluffs and mountains to either side and the river running through them, and with his arms outstretched he gazed upward at the sunset with that open, ecstatic expression on his face that arose only in moments of greatest joy. He stood like that for minutes.

CHAPTER EIGHT

FATHERS AND SONS

AS THE NORMAL retirement age of sixty-five came and went, Norman Maclean's popularity as a teacher resulted in repeated offers of a contract extension from the university until he voluntarily stepped down at age seventy. He said that decision was stimulated by his children, who had told him to live by his own maxim and quit before he wore out his welcome. Advanced age seemed to foreclose a follow-on career, but his sense of being unfulfilled, of a missed destiny, drove him onward. In a way, he had found freedom. As a widower and retiree, he could come and go as he pleased, when he pleased, answering only to himself. And that was the problem. Unseen voices still reached out to him, pressing him, urging him on, and as he said at the end of the book he ultimately wrote, *he reached back to them.*

In a 1972 letter to Robert Utley, his longtime friend and at one time chief historian for the National Park Service, he described the turning point. "In December I shall reach my Biblical allotment of three score years plus 10 (Jesus, isn't that appalling?). A good time to quit, don't you think? I'll resign next month to be effective in June when I have finished the school year. I'd rather not teach than not to teach well. Then I'll try a little writing. The summer before last I started some stories based on my memories of hunting and fishing and working in logging camps and for the Forest Service when I was young and when Montana and Idaho were younger than they are now. I think the stories are pretty good. The one I worked on last summer I didn't get finished. It is on the year when I was 17 years old and the United States Forest Service was 14. It got long and difficult (almost novelette size) and I had to start it four times before I liked the feel of it, but I hope to finish it this winter quarter when I don't teach."

That story became "USFS 1919: The Ranger, the Cook and a Hole in the Sky."

He continued in another letter to Utley in the fall of 1974: "The story I am finishing up now is in memory of my brother, who was one of the great fly fishermen of his time and who was murdered when he was 32. Its secondary intention should be clear, to give someone a knowledge of and feeling for the art—from rods and flies to casting, to 'reading water,' to landing (and losing) fish. Naturally it means a great deal to me, but I have tried not to make it too personal. In any event, when I finish it I believe I should stop, look and listen, and maybe ultimately stop. The three stories add up to a certain body of writing—a sufficient body to decide whether I am largely wasting the mornings of my remaining years in writing. I would rather spend my time fly fishing than in writing a mediocre story about fishing because I am better than mediocre as a fisherman."

ONE STORMY FALL day not long after that letter was written, we spent a family weekend together in another cabin, this one on the eastern shore of Lake Michigan that belonged to a family friend. We called it a cabin, but it was a frame two-bedroom summer house, painted white and typical of the Midwest, sited high on a sandy bluff with a broad view of the lake. The storm whipped across Lake Michigan and battered the house, but we had a fire going in the fireplace and the house was snug. The storm, though, kept us from our favorite pastime of hiking the beach and neighboring hardwood forests.

The weekend had just started when my father shyly handed my wife, Frances, and me the typescript of a long story he'd written. Frances and I had already read and commented on several other stories my father had written after he had taken up the pen virtually full-time following his retirement from the university. We were both working journalists at the time, and my father had done serious re-writing based on our comments; we figured we were in for another editing experience. Our marriage a few years ear-lier, in 1968, had been a Romeo and Juliet affair between two feuding houses: Frances was a feature writer for the *Chicago Sun-Times*, which was my paper, the *Tribune*'s, main competitor. Bob Wiedrich, a friend and mentor at the *Tribune*, had announced the nuptials in his Tower Ticker column with a double-edged remark: "Good luck, kids!" (The marriage has endured for over half a century.)

The typescript my father handed us that day was titled *A River Runs through It*, which made me wonder. What was an undefined "it" doing in a title? My wife and I took the story into our bedroom and, with the storm keeping us inside and the story being just over a hundred pages, we both read it through during the course of the day. And then we looked each other in the eye. "This sounds just like the books we used to read in literature class in college," Frances said. "The classics." God Almighty, I thought, she's right.

We took the manuscript and walked quietly back into the main room of the cabin, where my father awaited our reaction in an easy chair by the fire. He didn't look easy. He was hopeful and vulnerable in a way I'd never seen him look before. We told him just what we thought, that the story was perfect as it stood, no editing required. I told him I hadn't read anything so good since Shakespeare, and I hadn't read anything so authentic about fishing since he had introduced me long before to Hemingway's best fishing story, "Big Two-Hearted River."

"Don't let an editor change a word," I said.

Neither Frances nor I could put into our own words the effect of those final, magical paragraphs of his, but looks communicate, and we knew he understood what we were feeling, something more than words. He sat back in the chair, relieved and gratified. He'd especially liked the admiring comparison to Hemingway.

When I got around to asking about the "it" in the title, he answered simply. "It's the way a farmer might describe a river in one of his fields." He'd had a long and distinguished career as a professor of English and was about to become a famous author, but he was also a man who listened to the radio in Chicago for market prices on crops and livestock.

He was past seventy, but instead of fading out, Norman Maclean on that stormy day was on the cusp of fulfilling a lifetime ambition. He'd found no lasting satisfaction in his early writing, with the exception of the many letters he'd written to colleagues, friends, and family, and a few short pieces for special occasions. Early in his teaching career he'd written two essays included in *Critics and Criticism: Ancient and Modern,* an influential book of literary criticism edited by Ronald Crane, the head of the university's English department, and that had finished him for scholarly writing. He ended the "publish or perish" debate for himself with a rhetorical question, "Does the world need another article on lyric poetry?"

Instead, each spring in Chicago, when he could be certain of returning to Montana, he had let winter-repressed memories thaw out, and lying in his bed just before and after sleep, he'd fished the river he knew by heart, hole by hole. He was spartan and the reveries were short. "All the years when I was teaching at the University of Chicago, come summer when all the big scholars were going over to the British Museum, standing outside talking to each other and letting the pigeons shit on them from the roof, I was out here in Montana. I knew one thing—in the summer get back to Montana."

After all those decades, now came the payoff.

WE'D TOLD HIM in the cabin on the shore of Lake Michigan that *A River Runs through It* was perfect, but was it a book? At one hundred four pages it was too short for a novel, a bit too long for a short story, too close to real life for fiction, too fictionalized for autobiography. Much of it was familiar from the stories my father used to tell my sister and me when we were children, as he noted in the book's dedication: "To Jean and John, to whom I have long told stories." But events of several summers had been compressed into one and locales switched around to satisfy dramatic need. He'd moved the iconic Oxford Saloon from Missoula to Hamilton in the Bitterroot Valley for a climactic scene in one story, because he didn't want to break up the narrative by having the characters jump in a truck and make the drive to Missoula. Neal, the title story's no-good brother-in-law, performed the misdeeds of several people. Norman's brother Paul had acquired a glowing patina that well exceeded his mixed reputation in real life.

The world knows how it turned out. The story anchored *A River Runs through It and Other Stories,* published by the University of Chicago Press as its first-ever work of fiction, but only after two East Coast publishers had turned it down. One house replied that it wasn't in a genre they published. An editor for Alfred A. Knopf, Inc., however, wrote, "I suppose one could say that he's written the wrong book, especially for one who writes as well as he does." *A River Runs through It* was "a nice book but not a saleable book," one of the great misjudgments in the history of book publishing. (The legend that it was rejected because an East Coast publisher complained "it has trees in it" is often repeated, but it never happened. That phrase was a casual observation by one of Norman's followers from the East Coast, and it was merely a statement to explain away the rejections.)

The Knopf letter, though, was a lucky day for a young editor at the University of Chicago Press, Allen N. Fitchen. He had read the book and desperately wanted to publish it, but the U of C Press had a hard-and-fast rule against publishing original fiction. Fitchen devised a scheme to get around the rule by playing on regional resentments: he set out to get the book rejected in the East. Fitchen, assuming the role of Norman's agent, offered the book to Knopf in hopes it would be kicked back, which would give him a sympathy card with the Press's publications board. To use one of my father's favorite phrases, the Knopf letter floated into Fitchen's outstretched hands "like a feather from God."

Fitchen said, years later, "For those of us in love with the 'little book,' the letter from Knopf was heaven-sent— our signal to spring into action, to marshal our forces in making the case for publication to the Chicago faculty governing board of the U of C Press. We had a lot going for us in that three of Norman's greatest admirers were also three of the most distinguished, most intelligent, and most articulate members of the English department—Wayne Booth, Gwin Kolb, and Ned Rosenheim."

Kolb's opinion of the manuscript, written for the Press before the book had been accepted for publication, is a more perceptive analysis of it than much of what came after publication. "In his collection of stories, Norman Maclean has realized four distinct though related ends. First, he has produced a group of superb tales, tightly constructed and masterfully written, which mix hilarious comedy, poignant seriousness, and an unusually rich understanding of human nature. Secondly, he has recorded the partial autobiography of a remarkable man and teacher, tough, benevolent, sensitive, wise, sophisticated but direct and open. Thirdly, he has described the crafts of fly fishing and forestry with such grace and gusto that the most untutored reader is steadily absorbed and delighted. And finally, he has vividly and compellingly recreated a vanishing way and mood of life in the huge tract of land called the American West. Any one of these achievements would make the collection deserving of publication. The combination has produced an extraordinary book which certainly approximates the unique and which cries out for distribution to a wide audience."

The Press brought out *A River Runs through It and Other Stories* in 1976, shepherded at each stage by the author. He'd collected visual materials from the Forest Service and other sources in Montana while writing the book, and he passed them on as inspiration to Robert Williams, an illustrator and book designer with the Press. Williams created scratchboard drawings including a fat trout, which my dad said "looked like a damn Gefilte Fish." Williams went back to the drawing board, and then produced a series of illustrations that met the author's approval, but none has an image of a trout.

Careful readers over the years have tried diligently to match Williams's cover drawing of a river running beneath a high cliff to a landscape described in the book or anywhere in real-life Montana. Contacted in retirement in Chicago, where he had stayed on in the university's Hyde Park neighborhood, Williams said he had looked at Norman's collection of photos and drawings and created scenes based on those, aiming for the feel of wood engravings. As best he remembered, the cover scene is an imaginative composite, just as many thought it must be. Williams said he chose the color blue for the cover because of its association with water, but he regrets that the ink for the first couple of printings faded badly.

My father loved the quiet dignity of the first edition of the book, including Williams's illustrations, and he fondly referred to it as the Little Blue Book. The first printing in

1976 came to barely over fifteen hundred copies, but demand was high and a second printing of about thirty-five hundred copies was run off that same year. (Both of the first year's printings are identifiable by a typographical error that appears on page 27, line 15: the word *adways*. This was corrected to "always" in the third and all subsequent print runs. The true first printing can be identified by an additional and often overlooked error on the publisher's page, where the ISBN number is incorrectly given as 022650051, omitting the final 5 from the correct number, 0226500551, which appears in all subsequent printings.)

The Press had taken a big chance on the book and everyone awaited the reviews. The first was written by Nick Lyons for the spring 1976 issue of *Fly Fisherman* magazine. Lyons and my father did not know each other, but they had much in common. Lyons was an English professor at Hunter College—and he also was a fisherman and arguably the dean of fly-fishing writers. Lyons put his own considerable reputation on the line when he called the book a literary "classic" and "an uncanny blending of fly fishing with the affections of the heart." My father immediately wrote Lyons a letter on a personal level that was unusual for him, explaining why he'd written the book.

"I am deeply touched by your review of my stories in the Fly Fisherman's Bookshelf," he wrote. "I should like to think that the story, *A River Runs through It*, is somewhere near as good as you say it is, not so much for my sake as for the memory of my brother whom I loved and still do not understand, and could not help. Since you wrote so beautifully about the story, I feel that I must speak personally of it to you.

"After my father's death, there was no one—not even my wife—I could talk to about my brother and his death. After my retirement from teaching, I felt that it was imperative I come to some kind of terms with his death as part of trying to do the same with my own. This was the major impulse that started me to write stories at 70, and the first one naturally that I wrote was about him. It was both a moral and artistic failure. It was really not about my brother—it was only about how I and my father and our duck dogs felt about his death. So I put it aside. I wrote the other stories to get more confidence in myself as a story-teller and to talk out loud to myself about him. The story, which now stands as the first one in the book, is actually the last one I wrote. I hope it will be the best one (although not the last one) I ever write, and I thank you again for writing beautifully about it."

A short time later while attending an academic conference in New York City, where Nick Lyons lived, my father picked up a phone and invited himself over. This, too, was not like him.

"He called me up and asked if he could come by and meet me," Lyons said, when I contacted him about the meeting many years later. Lyons had helped me get started as an author, among other things introducing me to his daughter, Jennifer, my longtime literary agent. When he and I spoke, Lyons said he'd felt privileged that the University of Chicago Press had sent galleys of the book to a fly-fishing magazine, which had given him the chance to review it. He also had been surprised and pleased when Norman called him directly. When Norman arrived at his house, they'd sat down together and talked for hours about books, fishing, teaching, and life in general. It was the start of a lifelong friendship.

When I asked Lyons why he'd taken such an instant liking to *A River*, he said it was simply the book's obvious literary merit. "Any great piece of writing begins with the writing. I've heard that first paragraph a hundred times and it's never become a cliché. It's clear, sharp, brilliant writing. The book has a deep reverence for life; it comes from the heart. I fell in love with it. I've read the book three or four times, always with a sense of wonder."

A River Runs through It was the leading finalist for the Pulitzer Prize for fiction in 1976, but the Pulitzer board declined to award a prize in that category that year, on grounds there were no "distinguished" entries. Many years later Michael Miner, a well-regarded writer for the *Chicago Reader,* wrote a story wondering if Pulitzers couldn't be awarded retroactively, once a clear injustice was established, and he used *A River* as a prime example. His piece in the December 12, 2003, issue of the *Reader* included an accurate account of the case of *A River,* and since I had played a minor but contentious role in it, I've drawn on Miner's article for much of this account.

The Pulitzer jury for fiction that year was chaired by Herman Kogan, book editor for the *Chicago Sun-Times.* Kogan's jury put *A River Runs through It* at the top of their recommended list, Miner reported. "It's qualities are copious," Kogan wrote in his cover letter. "The range of emotions and insights is broad and compelling and its concern with life in all its aspects has, despite the narrative's specific time and place, a sense of the universal."

When no prize was awarded for fiction that year, Kogan was outraged. "Herman was absolutely beside himself," recalled his son Rick Kogan, a *Tribune* writer and editor, when Miner contacted him. "He had known Norman a very long time, but it was certainly not a matter of cronyism." A Pulitzer administrator explained in the *New York Times* that it had been a "thin year" for fiction and no book "was clearly leading the pack." Clayton Kirkpatrick, editor of the *Chicago Tribune* and a member of the Pulitzer board, was quoted in the *Times* story saying the nominees "were not as distinguished as we would have liked."

"This remark caught the eye of one of Kirkpatrick's reporters," Miner noted. "John Maclean was both a Washington correspondent for the *Tribune* and Norman Maclean's son. He immediately wrote Kirkpatrick, someone he greatly admired."

I can report that Miner's phrase "caught the eye" is an understatement. The *Tribune* had not reviewed *A River* when it appeared, a major failure for a notable book by a Chicago author. Not only that, but now the paper's editor—my boss—had dirtied up my dad in the *New York Times*, of all places: it's difficult to overstate the resentment "Second City" Chicagoans harbor for New York City. I marked "personal" on the envelope of my letter to Mr. Kirkpatrick, which is what we all called him out of respect.

"If the *Times* quoted you correctly about the lack of 'distinguished entries' I am saddened," I wrote. "There may be no grave injustice in denying the prize to *A River Run through It and Other Stories* by Norman Maclean, my father. It was a first work and of short stories at that. Few books get so far with those drawbacks. But the book overcame other obstacles as well. East Coast publishers refused to touch it. They didn't think a book with trees in it would interest readers [*sic*]. Then the tiny University of Chicago Press took it on as their first ever work of fiction. They are so small, though, that they cannot keep bookstores supplied. Despite all that, the book caught on. It outsells Saul Bellow's *Humboldt's Gift* at the U of C Bookstore. Reviewers have praised its literary merit in major publications such as *The New York Review of Books*, the *New York Times*, *Newsweek*, *Publishers Weekly*, the *Chicago Sun-Times*, the *Chicago Daily News* and literally dozens of others. An exception was the *Chicago Tribune*, which ignored it.

"I recount this history because it seemed so unnecessary to have the book called undistinguished. I submit it has distinguished itself in many ways without the help of the Pulitzer, East Coast publishers, or the *Chicago Tribune*."

Mr. Kirkpatrick wrote me back, also marking his envelope "personal." He acknowledged that the *Tribune* should have reviewed the book, but said the Pulitzer board had taken a vote and that was that. Mr. Kirkpatrick was one of the most decent men I've ever known, and I never suffered a penalty at the *Tribune* for writing to him as I did.

My dad, as can be guessed, was absolutely delighted with my letter.

Success is welcomed at any age, but *A River* came out the year my father turned seventy-four years old and it exalted him and propelled him forward as a writer and a public personality. A bright future seemed about to open up, one filled with more books, book signings, invitations to speak, and other joys of literary fame. He even seemed bigger physically, walking with a strut and speaking in a voice of renewed authority. He figured he'd quickly follow his first success with a nonfiction narrative about another Montana story, the Mann Gulch Fire. He'd been incubating that tale for decades since visiting the site of the fire, and getting it down on paper shouldn't take long. Then how about a book about great women of the West, he thought. Women got stuck in the back seat in a lot of Western storytelling, but he'd known western women of outstanding qualities and accomplishments, whose stories needed telling. The possibilities seemed endless, and indeed perks began to shower down.

When he returned to Montana one summer soon after *A River* came out, he was invited to speak before the Rocky Mountain Institute, a research institution in Missoula. More than two hundred people gathered at the Florence Hotel, the city's finest, to welcome him home. When he was young, he'd paid his way into the Wilma Theatre near the hotel building to watch vaudeville acts; now he was the featured entertainer in the hotel's Governor's Room. He gleefully thanked the gathering for giving him the "cover" to reengage as a Montanan after a half-century as "Robert

Hutchins's Shakespearian voice," referring to the man who'd publicly teased him over his Ph.D. diploma—and been his longtime supporter.

He then settled down to research the Mann Gulch Fire, staying at the cabin and visiting the archives in the Forest Service's Region 1 headquarters building in Missoula. He quickly reestablished ties to his old agency. His stories about his adventures in the early years of the Forest Service recounted in *A River* gave him as much recognition and respect in the Forest Service as the story about fishing had done with the fly-fishing community. The USFS public affairs staff assigned Laird Robinson, who had been a USFS smokejumper foreman and now worked for public affairs at the Region 1 office, to help him with the research, and thereby established a bond that lasted the rest of their lives. Norman and Laird made several trips into Mann Gulch together, and for one of them my dad located the two living survivors, Bob Sallee and Walt Rumsey, and brought them back for a field trip, among other things restoring their once close friendship. All seemed to be going well for him and the Mann Gulch project. And then trouble struck.

My father's formal writing style in books and for other publications was what he called "noble prose," and he found that a straightforward, journalistic reconstruction of the

Mann Gulch Fire wasn't working for him. After struggling for several years, he handed a draft manuscript of the book to his first editor, Allen Fitchen, who told him frankly that he'd made a hash of it. "It was a bad book," Fitchen said when I asked him about it years later. My father did not take criticism of this kind with good grace, and his relationship with Fitchen was never the same after that. But others told my father the same thing, and so he took it to heart. He realized he needed to take an entirely different approach and treat the story as tragedy, which he had long taught was the highest form of literature. So he set out to make the transition, which was more like an utter transformation, and the job lasted the rest of his long life and beyond.

He still had to get the facts straight, though, and Laird Robinson took on the role of "Norman's research partner," a title he cherished—and deserved. But the story was tying my father in knots. I'd call him from Washington, D.C., and ask him how things were going. Mann Gulch, he said, was "a cloud by day and a pillar of fire by night." The biblical reference from the Book of Exodus, describing how the Lord led the Israelites out of Egypt, well described the way the Mann Gulch story beckoned my father on, by day and by night, always out of reach. He worked on it from the cabin in Montana as many months as the weather allowed, clear into the stormy weather of November, and he hardly took time out to fish. George Croonenberghs told him to "toss that book in the closet and let's go fish the Blackfoot." But he could not let it go.

DURING THIS PERIOD, I lived a divided life of my own in Washington, D.C., similar to the family life that I'd experienced as a youngster ferrying back and forth between the West and Midwest. After moving to the East in 1970 to join the *Tribune's* Washington bureau, my wife, Frances, our two sons, Dan and John Fitzroy, and I discovered in the new surroundings an easily accessible outdoor life; in my family, we learn as much from the land as we do from books. We could hike and canoe virtually in the city, in Rock Creek Park or along the C&O Canal or the Potomac River, and nearby mountains offered greater opportunities including fly fishing. I even wrote a poem about our favorite family spot, up in the mountains of Virginia.

The Rapidan River rises high
In the Blue Ridge Mountains,
Up with the black bears and Eastern Brook Trout,
And of all the lovely little rivers
That start up there in the clouds
It is perhaps the most beautiful.

We kept connected to Montana, but it was a long haul and the visits were irregular. We made the trip by car one summer, but it amounted to a week on the road each way, so flying became the preferred way to go. The link to Montana may have been intermittent, but it was a vital one. Dan went on to attend the University of Montana, graduated with a degree in geology, and then worked in the oil patch in eastern Montana for several years, where on days off he hunted for—and found—petrified dinosaur eggs. He then headed to Alaska, becoming probably the first person in history, as he remarked, to move to that state for a better climate, an improved social life, and to get the hell away from the oil business. He's the author of *Paddling the Yukon River and Its Tributaries*, for which he spent four summers canoeing those waters single-handed: Alaska summers are short and the rivers long. He's since become chair of the science department at Robert Service High School in Anchorage, where he lives with his wife, Kristiann, and three children, Bronwyn, Paisley Kathleen, and Larsen Muir, and helps feed his family with rod and gun.

My younger son, John Fitzroy, whom we call John-Fitz, and I came west together and joined my father at the cabin several times during the years he was at work on the Mann Gulch story. My dad was in his early eighties, but he still drove alone to Montana from Chicago. After a stint at the City News Bureau, JohnFitz had been a reporter at the *Montgomery Advertiser* in Montgomery, Alabama, covering among other things a cross burning by the Ku Klux Klan in the southeastern corner of the state. But he was headed for law school. He went on to become a public defender for the state of Maryland, working in the division defending juveniles, and established his own family, his wife, Amy; daughter, Ashlyn; and son, Evan Fitzroy.

The first time JohnFitz, my dad, and I were at the cabin together, we decided to take a hike to Morrell Lake at the headwaters of Morrell Creek. The lake is a wonder spot. You can look from there to the tops of the rugged Swan Range that form the western edge of the Bob Marshall Wilderness. That's where Morrell Creek gets its start, up around seven thousand feet where snow and ice can last into August. The creek comes down the mountains in a dramatic series of waterfalls, and the last one right before Morrell Lake is big and picturesque.

Back in the old days, when my dad was young, he'd had to hike more than twenty miles to reach Morrell Lake. But as logging roads extended into the backcountry, the trailhead moved closer to the lake and the hike shortened. By the time the three of us walked into the lake, the trail was down to about two and a half miles. On that trip we found a makeshift raft pulled up on the lakeshore, left by a previous outfit. Those remote mountain lakes are often ringed by timber and difficult to fish from shore, and fishermen who build rafts out of driftwood or fallen logs often leave them for the next group.

JohnFitz was too young to have taken up fly fishing, but he happily got on the raft and draped the harness of my wicker fishing basket over his shoulders. I waded out pulling the raft, using it as a float when we reached deep water, and hung on to the raft with one hand while casting with the other. When I caught a fish, I flopped it onto the raft, and JohnFitz unhooked it and put it in the basket. He was content as keeper of the fish. My dad sat on a log on the shore and he was happy, too, watching me fish in this odd manner with his grandson. I caught a gorgeous mess of cutthroat trout, the ones with the lush Morrell Creek coloring.

The next time we went to Morrell Lake we were all older by several years, and I should have been wiser. Once again, the three of us were at the cabin and looking for something fun to do together. I didn't give it a second thought and said, "Why don't we all hike into Morrell Lake like we did last time and do a little fishing?"

You have to get to the lake early for the morning rise, because the fish stop biting by about one o'clock. The water's so cold your lower parts go numb if there's no raft and you need to wade, which was the case this time. You need to arrive early, fish, and get out of the water promptly. We'd timed it just right, and when we arrived at the lake a general rise was under way. All across the lake, expanding circles of wavelets appeared on the barely rippled water as trout did a "head poke" or just sipped to take flies from the surface. It was a compelling sight as a new rise form, as they're called, instantly came to life for every one that flattened and died out. I waded out and caught all I wanted in a short time: it was only a few, because by then I was working my way into the catch-and-release ethic.

JohnFitz stayed on the bank to keep my dad company. My father sat on a log looking happy but tired. I waded back to shore and offered my father the rod. "Dad, do you want to fish for a while?" I said. "It's still early, the fish are still moving."

He had this wonderful smile on his face, one that came from deep within and lit up the world. "I don't need to do any fishing," he said. "Let's just hike out."

We took it easy on the return trip and all went well until about the halfway point. My father by then was leaning backward, tipping back at an alarming angle. He tried to smile, but his face was a grimace and he was having trouble making headway. We had about a mile to go.

"Go right along with him and talk to him, see what you can do," I told my son.

JohnFitz already was helping him, without seeming to

do it. He put a supporting hand on his grandfather's back, not pushing but just encouraging him along, talking to him, letting him stop whenever he needed to rest. It got rough toward the end, but JohnFitz was tender and patient with him, and we made it back to the trailhead without serious mishap.

"He's a tough old bird, he did well," JohnFitz said to me.

My father sat down heavily in the car's passenger seat. "I'd like to go back to the cabin and have a rest," he said. So that's what we did. We'd left the gate closed on the short dirt road to the cabin, and when we turned onto the dirt JohnFitz offered to jump out and open the gate. Norman wasn't having it. "I'll do it," he said, and stepped out and opened the gate. Once inside the cabin, though, he had a lie-down.

And that was the last fishing trip. The very last one.

REDFORD'S MOVIE OF *A River Runs Through It*, which premiered two years after my father's death in 1990, at the age of eighty-seven, extended the book's reach beyond the literary and fly-fishing worlds, where it had become a cult favorite, to a general audience in countries all over the world. Fans of the book weren't entirely satisfied with the movie, but it's a rare film that a whole family can watch and enjoy together as they can this one. There's plenty of adult drama in the movie. The kids who see it are drawn to Paul, and most recognize that his behavior is going to catch up with him—and they don't have to witness his unhappy ending.

Philippe Rousselot won the Oscar for cinematography, the photographic art that "paints poetry that sears our hearts and lingers in our minds," as Morgan Freeman described it in making the award to him in 1993. The movie's compelling depiction of fly fishing sparked a global mania for the sport. Fisherfolk dressed in fresh-from-the-box Stetson hats and vests, just like the guys in the movie, cropped up on rivers everywhere. As they crowded onto Montana rivers, the Blackfoot River became a heavily trafficked "must" stop. Fishing guides, with business doubling and redoubling, called it simply "The Movie."

The success of the film, though, had a double and contrary effect on the Blackfoot. The river had become so severely degraded by the time the movie premiered in 1992 that Montana Fish, Wildlife and Parks didn't bother making fish counts. "We all know about the high jumping, hard fighting rainbow trout of the Blackfoot River that enlivened scenes in *A River Runs through It*," said David Brooks, executive director of Montana Trout Unlimited. "By the 1980s, not even Paul could have coaxed such a fish from those waters."

The Blackfoot had suffered a major blow in 1975 when

the Mike Horse Dam, located on the western slope of Rogers Pass at the river's headwaters, burst and sent tons of toxic mine waste down the river. The dam became a Superfund site, but for years the water was fouled and the fishery devastated. We stopped fishing there for several years, until healthier water levels returned. In the 1980s, Trout Unlimited put down seed money to restart fish surveys and identify the most urgent problems, notably overharvesting and degradation of tributaries by mining, grazing, logging, and roads. Then the movie came along, spawning a fly-fishing craze with an amazing reach; it broke out in Japan, for example, which has no trout fishery to speak of. The movie also brought an outpouring of donations and support for the Blackfoot that made an "astonishing" difference in the river's health, according to Brooks.

Two organizations, the Big Blackfoot Chapter of Trout Unlimited and the Blackfoot Challenge, worked with landowners, individual donors, and state and federal agencies to address the problems. The money that poured in could move quickly to projects, because it did not have to navigate a lengthy governmental review process. By Brooks's reckoning, over five hundred projects of various kinds were undertaken, including more than seventy-five restoration efforts that cost about $15 million. Thirty or more tributaries were cleaned up and reconnected to the Blackfoot: one particularly meaningful project restored water flow to Belmont Creek, which had become a dry creek in summer before it reached the Blackfoot, at the place near where Norman, Paul, and the Reverend Maclean fished together for the last time. "The heart of the Blackfoot recovery story is that it has been driven by local participation," Brooks said. The close relationship among donors of all kinds, conservation groups, and local landowners and other stakeholders has made the Blackfoot a national model for river restoration.

Another challenge arose during the late 1990s, a few years after the movie came out, when a Colorado mining firm made plans for an enormous open-pit, cyanide leach operation near Lincoln and the river's headwaters to mine an estimated four million ounces of gold. The ensuing protest against the McDonald Project caused headlines like this one: Will a Mine Run through It? The state canceled the mineral lease in 2000 and eventually the company walked away, after an epic battle recounted in Richard Manning's *One Round River: The Curse of Gold and the Fight for the Big Blackfoot.*

The river also gained from the deliberate removal of another dam, the Milltown Dam on the Clark Fork at the mouth of the Blackfoot, which blocked trout from getting up the Blackfoot to spawn. Uncounted tons of toxic mine waste from operations upriver at Butte and Anaconda piled up behind the dam following its completion in 1908. An alarm sounded in 1980 when arsenic was discovered in the drinking water of a few residents who lived adjacent to the Milltown Dam and reservoir. The removal project joined two other cleanup sites and became the Clark Fork River Superfund Complex, eventually growing into the nation's largest and most costly Superfund cleanup. The movie helped "move the needle toward dam removal," Brooks said, because people wanted the Blackfoot returned to its legendary fishing glory. It took decades to accomplish. The dam wasn't completely removed until 2008, and restoration work continued for several years after that. "After spring high water subsided in 2014, the Blackfoot and Clark Fork confluence was fully open to all floaters for the first time in more than a century," Brooks concluded in *Restoring the Shining Waters: Superfund Success at Milltown, Montana.*

The way was now open for fish as well as floaters to move between the two rivers. For the Blackfoot, this has meant more big fish like the enormous one I hooked in the Muchmore Hole, just a few years after the dam was removed. The Clark Fork is simply bigger water that supports bigger fish—and now they can swim up the Blackfoot and access their historic spawning grounds.

The Blackfoot was more remote and certainly less well known than the Clark Fork, at least until the movie made it famous. It used to be what fishing guides called a "tomahawk" or secondary river: few anglers asked for it and few guides used it, except as an alternative when bigger rivers like the Clark Fork and Missouri weren't producing. Even in those days, my father complained about the "Spanish Armada" that came tumbling down the Blackfoot on inner tubes, rafts, and other watercraft, tossing out beer cans along the way: in fairness, the Armada included a large number of college students and other frolickers using the lower Blackfoot near Missoula to keep cool on hot summer days. But the flotilla of guide boats had started to arrive in his time, too.

Today, many anglers coming to Montana put a Blackfoot River float near the top of their agendas, according to Paul Roos, who had a fly-fishing shop in Helena but built a resort for fishermen on the North Fork of the Blackfoot after the movie came out. "Guests stay in well-appointed canvas tent cabins with first-class meals served in a well-appointed lodge overlooking spring fed ponds and the North Fork of the Blackfoot River," according to the operation's current website (Roos, who had a distinguished career not only as an outfitter but also as an advocate for the Blackfoot River and other conservation causes, died in November 2020 at the age of 78.) Others, too, have sited luxury accommodations on the river's banks, using the Blackfoot's literary legacy to launch a new armada that makes the older one look modest by comparison.

Jay Proops, whose ranch has extensive riverfront, says that on summer days he's counted as many as seventy rigs with boat trailers parked at the Harry Morgan Fishing Access Site on the North Fork, a popular starting point for a float on the upper Blackfoot, and more than twice as many campers as campsites. That many rigs from just one launch site would be a gross overburden even for bigger water like the Madison or the Missouri. Some guides simply skip the holes on the North Fork and the first ones on the Blackfoot, Proops says, and float directly to the Muchmore Hole, where they allow clients to fish for hours before moving on. Fishermen have been observed using treble hooks that can cause trout much injury. Trespassers also come through his ranchland to fish, taking a chance in a state where the Second Amendment is revered. Talk of self-regulation by the guide community has gone virtually nowhere. The state imposes regulations on other waters—limiting float trips on the Smith and Big Hole rivers, for example—but for some reason has failed to address the problems of the Blackfoot. Overuse and other unsportsmanlike practices are the major challenges facing the river today. The Blackfoot has survived challenges in the past, but its celebrity status has come at a price.

CHAPTER NINE

TOUCHED BY FIRE

AFTER THIRTY-PLUS YEARS in the news business I felt
a tug from the West that became irresistible. It came on
July 6, 1994, when fourteen firefighters including three
smokejumpers were killed in the South Canyon Fire on
Storm King Mountain in central Colorado. It was the first
time smokejumpers had died from flames since the Mann
Gulch Fire, forty-five years earlier. In many ways, the
Storm King event was Mann Gulch all over again. Once
again a fire had mushroomed like an atomic explosion
in a narrow canyon above a river big enough to share the
name of a state—the Colorado in Colorado, the Missouri
in Montana. Once again shouts of "Let's get the hell out
of here!" had echoed ahead of engulfing smoke and flame.
Once again more than a dozen firefighters had been lost,

and once again, there was sadness and blame on an epic scale.

While the fire still burned and the search continued for the last bodies, an editor at the *Tribune*, Owen Youngman, came over to my desk with a questioning look on his face.

News accounts from Colorado highlighted the similarities between the Mann Gulch and South Canyon fires, and many mentioned *Young Men and Fire,* which had appeared just two years earlier, in 1992, the same year as the release of the movie of *A River.* After our father's death in 1990, my sister, Jean, and I had taken the unfinished manuscript to the University of Chicago Press, and then worked with the Press to get the book over the last hurdles to publication. Alan Thomas, the book's editor, wrote a Publisher's Note about the process, partly to forestall the idea that we rewrote the book for Norman. Thomas noted that the editing and fact-checking did not alter the book's basic structure, and the words and vision are my father's. By the time of the fire on Storm King Mountain, the book already had made smokejumpers and wildland fire familiar to a broad general public, and not incidentally created a timeless work for the wildland fire community.

The natural thing would have been for Youngman to dispatch me to Colorado on the next plane to cover the unfolding story of the South Canyon Fire, but he waited to see if I had any ideas of my own. After a moment's thought, I told him, "If I go to Colorado now, I'll be chasing the story a couple of days behind reporters for the Associated Press and the local newspapers, and you'll wind up with a Maclean byline on a story that's a lot like wire service copy. Everybody says this fire is a repeat of the Mann Gulch Fire. Why don't we find out? Why don't I go to Mann Gulch? The anniversary is coming up in August. I'll bet I can get my dad's research partner Laird Robinson and some others to go along, for different perspectives."

"Okay, do it," Youngman said.

Less than a month later on August 5, the forty-fifth anniversary of the Mann Gulch Fire, a small group of us made our way into the gulch, looking for an answer to the question, why hadn't the loss of thirteen smokejumpers there prevented a similar tragedy in Colorado? Laird Robinson had taken a day off from work at the Forest Service to make the trip; other recruits included a retired National Park Service administrator, a young English professor, an insurance man from Helena, and my cousin Bob Burns. We took my cousin's boat from the Gates of the Mountains Marina, six miles downstream, to the mouth of the gulch, where we disembarked and hiked from there. Mann Gulch is shaped like a funnel with the narrowest part at the Missouri River, where we landed. After a short walk, we reached the place

where R. Wagner "Wag" Dodge, the smokejumper foreman, had been surprised to see a ball of fire coming up the
gulch toward him and the smokejumpers he was leading
down to the river. He turned his men around and headed
back up the gulch, beginning what came to be called A
Race That Couldn't Be Won.

Higher up, the gulch opens into a broad amphitheater
surrounded at the top by a jutting wall of rimrock. Dodge
and his men entered the amphitheater with the fire clos-
ing fast behind them. It takes no special gift for fantasy
to imagine goblins sitting on those rocks gibbering with
glee as they watch young men scramble and fall on the im-
possibly steep hillsides below, chased by a wall of hellish
flame. Dodge saved himself by lighting a fire in front of
the advancing flames and lying down in its ashes, calling
on his men to join him. None did. Two men, Sallee and
Rumsey, ran up the side of Dodge's fire, using it as a buffer
to the main fire, and made it through the rimrock to safety.
Flames caught the others.

Much the same thing had happened in Colorado. There,
a group of firefighters had been caught by a fire that unexpectedly blew up below them in a narrow canyon. They
turned and scrambled along a sidehill to get out, and all
but one perished. Don Mackey, a Missoula smokejumper,
had been in charge of that section of fire line. Mackey first

directed a group of his fellow smokejumpers up a spur ridge to safety. He could have saved himself by joining them, which is what they expected him to do. Instead, he turned and went back along the fire line to join twelve other firefighters he had put in harm's way, and he died with them. The lone survivor from that group was Eric Hipke, a North Cascades smokejumper, whose hands were badly burned when the fire caught up to him as he made a final leap to safety at the top of the ridge. Two helitack crewmen, firefighters who work from a helicopter, that were not part of this group followed a separate path on the mountain and they, too, were caught by the fire, bringing the total loss to fourteen.

On our anniversary trip into Mann Gulch, we hiked to the top of the ridge near the gap where Sallee and Rumsey had broken through to safety. There, we sat down to take a breather and talk things over. We huffed and puffed and drank water. Below us on the hillside were scattered crosses, marking the places where men had fallen. The crosses were so small and hidden by grass that they could be overlooked at first. But curiously, once recognized for what they were, their stark, regular geometry and bone-white color fixed in the mind and they dominated the hillside.

What had been missed in Colorado? we wondered. The fourteen deaths on Storm King Mountain clearly meant something big had gone wrong. "I know exactly what your dad would have thought," Robinson said. "It would be the same as I felt when I heard about Storm King. He would have been outraged and angered, and then hurt and disappointed. He would have thought, 'How could they let that happen again?' He would have thought that one of the last things he achieved in his life—that Mann Gulch would never happen again—had been taken away." The Forest Service had adopted new safety measures after Mann Gulch that had saved many lives, notably the Ten Standard Orders for firefighting safety; several of the orders are linked to Mann Gulch, including the one that states: know what your fire is doing at all times. My father had been justified in believing that the fallen of Mann Gulch had not died in vain, but were, as he wrote, "often to be present in times of catastrophe helping to save the living" from a similar fate. That promise had been broken on Storm King Mountain.

Some of the firefighters at Storm King had escape routes, others did not. They were in heavy vegetation with no chance for an escape fire like Dodge's. They knew dangerous weather was on the way, but they hadn't received a key update that warned high winds would arrive much sooner than expected. Radio frequencies had jammed with traffic and turned into babble. "All the voices became equally meaningful or meaningless," remarked O. Alan Weltzien, a professor of English at the University of Montana Western in Dillon.

The firefighters could have pulled out to safety earlier, when the weather began to change, but those in our group who had fought fire said weather shifts are normal conditions for fighting fire in the summer. "If you pulled out every time a storm came up, you'd never put out a fire," they agreed. And young people by nature take on fires—literally and figuratively, as my father had described in *Young Men and Fire.* "What do you expect when you give young people a job like that?" said Jim Van Meter, a life insurance agent from Helena. "Young people think they can lick anything."

We left the gulch to its ghosts and walked out.

I wrote my story for the *Tribune* and thought I had done my duty to the newspaper, the fire service, and my father, and could carry on as before. Then I called Bob and Nadine Mackey, Don's parents, who lived in the Bitterroot Valley near Missoula. They were eager to talk about their son, who had been an extraordinary outdoorsman—a kind of throwback to the mountain men—and a storyteller and charmer who could connect with the young and the old, women and men. We talked about his decision to go back for others when he could have saved himself. "That was Don," they said without hesitation, and so did everyone I ever talked to who had known him.

As I thought about Don Mackey's decision, I admired the way he'd acted—selflessly and without hesitation. My own life, too, seemed to be headed for a turning point, and in my youth I'd dreamed of being the kind of modern-day mountain man Don had been. I had gone in a very different direction, however, and could only imagine what it had been like to be a smokejumper facing wind-driven flames on a mountainside. But when you've worked for thirty years at the same job, for the same employer, you should ask yourself, why am I still here? I'd had a good run and my résumé then could be boiled down to a single sentence: as diplomatic correspondent for the *Tribune*'s Washington bureau, I flew around the world with Secretary of State Henry Kissinger on his famed shuttle diplomacy trips. I'd started young in the news business, barely twenty-one years old, and had covered everything from Chicago race riots and street crime to the first moon landing to the fall of Richard Nixon and Watergate. The Kissinger shuttle, though, had dominated global headlines whenever it flew, back and forth between capitals in the Middle East to secure agreements between Egypt and Israel and on other missions. Richard Valeriani, who covered the shuttles for NBC, told the story of the "Kissinger 14," as they called the reporters who flew with the secretary of state, in his book *Travels with Henry*. Those of us who'd been on those flights shared our clips and memories with Valeriani for his book.

By early spring of the next year, 1995, Bob Mackey and I had agreed by phone to meet on Storm King Mountain and try to locate the place where his son had been standing when he had made his fateful decision to turn back. By then, I'd sent off a proposal to write a book about the fire and had made preliminary plans to leave the *Tribune*. Everything came together on the same day, even at the same hour: a book contract finalized and minutes later I signed papers to quit the *Tribune*. A few days later, on April Fool's Day, I stepped into my Jeep Cherokee and headed west to Colorado, hoping this wasn't all a big joke on me: at age fifty-two, I had a lot of work years ahead.

On a warm spring day on Storm King Mountain, Bob and I located the spot on a spur ridge where Don had made his decision to go back for "the people in the brush patch," as he called the dozen firefighters on the fire line. We could be sure of the place, because the fire line ended right at the top of the spur ridge. The crew had stopped work there and taken a lunch break just before the fire blew up. The smokejumpers Don had directed to safety remembered him standing there, at the head of the fire line. That's where he had turned and headed back for the others.

Bob and I found the place where we virtually could

stand in Don's boot prints at the time he'd made his decision. From there, you can see down to Interstate Highway 70 and a housing development in a meadow near the highway; urban stuff. But you're high above on an uninhabited ridge that's crisscrossed by game trails. You can also see the Colorado River below and mountains without number, the backbone of the Rocky Mountains, spread out on a broad horizon; the ridge has a wild and remote feel. We stood silently for a while, each with our own thoughts. Don Mackey's decision is a haunting one. The fire world today has a term for it, when someone knowingly turns and risks their life for others on a wildland fire: it's called a Don Mackey Moment.

My second career, writing about wildfire in the West, gave me the freedom to return for long stretches to the family cabin at Seeley Lake, where I often headquartered for field research. It was a strange sensation to live in the same cabin, cook in the same kitchen, and damn near freeze at night in the same bed my father had used when he had worked on the Mann Gulch Fire. The bed wasn't much more than an iron cot. I looked under the thin mattress one time and found newspapers from the 1970s that he'd stuffed there for insulation. From the lakeshore I could see the Seeley Lake Ranger Station at the far north end of the lake. It had been part of the Forest Service smokejumping program that resulted in the first operational jump in 1940; the training base was even closer, at Camp Paxson, just a short walk from our cabin; the airstrip the trainees used was a couple of miles down the road. The links to my father, his book, and smokejumping were everywhere around me. As a friend warned, "Whatever you write is going to be compared to *Young Men and Fire*."

At one point I had to make a decision about specifically acknowledging the father-son link. Just before the Colorado fire blew up, a Missoula smokejumper named Quentin Rhodes, who had been on the spur ridge with Mackey and survived, had remarked, "We're going to have to resurrect Norman Maclean to tell this story." Rhodes's quote appears in official documentation, and he confirmed it to me in an interview. It doesn't sound like a big deal now, but if I'd included it in my book *Fire on the Mountain* it would have required an awful lot of explaining—about my father, his book, myself, and my book. At the time I was struggling to establish an individual voice. I'd determined to keep myself out of the story and write a straightforward, short-on-the-frills account of the fire, and not try to imitate my father's more personal approach or writing style. It felt right back then, a quarter century ago, to leave out the Rhodes quote.

My book about the South Canyon Fire, *Fire on the*

Mountain, appeared in 1999, was well received, and led to another book and then another about fatal wildland fires. I squirmed around trying to find a different subject, but I kept getting calls from parents and friends of firefighters who had been lost in fires, saying, they're blaming the dead for what happened and they cannot speak for themselves. Can you come look into this? Sometimes the answer is yes, sometimes no, depending on the circumstances. At this point, a quarter century later, the number of books has reached half a dozen and counting.

ONCE I BEGAN spending long periods of time in the West, I had a lot of catching up to do as a fisherman. I'd tried to keep up back in the East, but it wasn't the same as regular fishing of Western waters. Meanwhile, the sport had undergone transformative changes in equipment and techniques. There was a time of learning for me, investing in better rods and reels, switching from wet flies to mostly dry flies, and learning different casting methods. I fell into a pattern when possible of writing in the morning, a habit I picked up from my dad, and then heading for the Blackfoot and other rivers, fly rod in hand, later in the day. I also made the full switchover to catch-and-release, an enlightened and necessary ethic for today's heavily used waters.

I caught an awful lot of fish, some of them good-sized: sixteen-, eighteen-, even twenty-inch trout that would have been the signature of a season when I was younger. They were beautiful trout, in that special larger sense, and fought many a good fight. But none was *the* big fish for me. Size counts, but in my family, fishing means more than catching fish that can be measured in inches and pounds. There has to somehow be a link to the past, a present moment of consequence, and God knows what all else to make it complete. We fish as a way to communicate with each other, living and dead. We fish to keep a present hold on Montana and to recall the frontier Eden it once was. We fish to compete against each other—living and dead. We fish because it's the family legacy, a demanding craft handed down from one generation to the next.

Late one afternoon at Seeley Lake, just a stone's throw from shore in front of the cabin, all these elements came together, wondrously and unexpectedly, and ended in a harsh awakening as dreams too often do. There'd been virtually no wind, not a murmur, for several days in a row and a magical stillness hung over the entire region. Seeley Lake was like glass and time seemed to stand still. It was October, traditionally a time of great fishing before the aspen and cottonwood leaves clutter the streams and freezing temperatures bring an end to insect hatches. The fish, energized by the cooling water, come eagerly to the surface to feed.

Day after day I drove over to the Blackfoot and fished favorite waters, but windless days and endless sunshine had put the fish down. I was being refused, as my father might have said, on home ground. Late one afternoon I sat in discouragement on the slope leading down from the cabin to the lake wondering how to change my luck. Scattered rise forms dotted the lake, just little kisses, not big splashes. There were lots of these rises close to shore where trout normally would feed on insect hatches coming off the lakeside brush. Seeley Lake was once a fine trout fishery, but it had been virtually ruined in the 1990s by the illegal and deeply stupid bucket dumping of northern pike in the Clearwater River drainage. The pike went crazy in Seeley Lake, annihilating trout, perch, largemouth bass, sunfish, frogs, snakes, and anything else they could get their teeth around. Wildlife populations trend in peaks and valleys, expanding until they exhaust habitat and forage and then abruptly pulling back or crashing. For a while, enormous pike that had gorged themselves in the lake of plenty were caught or speared, but as they slaughtered their food source the average size diminished. Even so, someone in 2010 yanked a thirty-pounder out of Seeley Lake that actually measured forty-four inches long. Northern pike are a great game fish in their native waters, but that's not Seeley Lake.

Something had to explain the rise forms I was watching, and pike are not surface feeders. I went for my rod. It took only a few paddle strokes in the canoe to get within casting distance of whatever those rise forms were. I shook out some line and cast a large dry fly into a concentric circle of wavelets, expanding outward from the center of a rise, and in the next instant felt what seemed like the bottom of the lake as it took the fly. The "it" dived in a swirl of bubbles like an escaping submarine, stripping line off my reel. It took me nearly a half hour to raise it close enough to the surface to see what it was. What I'd hooked was an enormous cutthroat trout, with its characteristic crimson slashes on the underside of the jaw.

I manhandled the cutthroat into the canoe. God almighty, it was big. Cutthroat normally are brightly colored, but this one was just a pale silver from jaw to tail. Very large trout were known to live in the depths of Seeley Lake, beyond the reach of either northern pike or the sun needed to give them color. The sunny windless days that had put down the fish in the Blackfoot River had apparently brought a remnant trout population up to the lake's surface to feed. I'd never seen or heard of a trout this size being caught on Seeley Lake, and certainly not on a dry fly. It was a winner, brought to hand within sight of the family cabin where ghosts of the past are ever-present—and keep score.

Cutthroat are a gentle species that normally lie still once they're out of the water, as though posing for a portrait. But the moment this one was in the canoe it began to thrash violently, its body slamming on the hull of the canoe. I snapped two quick shots with a pocket camera, and they show the fish in blurry mid-twist. Long moments passed as I subdued the fish, extracted the hook, and released the trout back to the lake. The great fish, suddenly unmoving, went down like a stone. It had accumulated too many years of easy living on the bottom of the lake, and the long fight and its thrashing around in the canoe had killed it. I was responsible, and not only had I killed the fish, but I had lost it, too. What an incredible waste! I paddled to shore, put up my rod, sat heavily down, and called Frances, who was holding the fort at home in the East. In an agony of remorse, I told her what had happened and we were sad together.

If that was the end of the story, it would be a sorry tale, especially for the fish, and not much more. Fortunately, matters took a different course.

Half a dozen years later I learned that a Seeley Lake neighbor and artisan, Jeff Wisehart, had taken up carving and assembling trout mounts. I showed him the two photos, which pictured not only the fish in the canoe but also a section of the fly rod. The fish in the photograph was twisting, but we still could compare it to the length of a pictured rod section, which could be measured exactly. We figured that cutthroat was twenty-eight to twenty-nine inches long, which would mean it weighed eight to nine pounds: a real lunker.

Jeff had never put together a mount as large as this, but it turned out he had a personal and inspiring link to the fish. "You caught that fish shortly after I had my heart attack and quintuple bypass surgery," he told me. "The fish died from a heart attack and, thanks be to God, I did not." He agreed to give it a try. Gathering materials, carving, joining parts and painting the mount took him six months. Jeff and his son-in-law, Sean Wildhaber, a firefighter with Montana's Bitterroot Hotshots, even managed to link the trout replica to wildland fire. Sean brought home a chunk of scorched juniper with chainsaw marks on it from a fire he'd fought, and Jeff incorporated it as the base for the mount. "Due to your involvement with wildland firefighters," Jeff noted, "it was a no-brainer." The trout body is carved of western cedar, the tail is redwood, and the fins are created from quaking aspen.

The trout photos show the telltale orange on the throat, but also show the lack of the distinctive brilliant hues. Jeff decided to make the model in high spawning colors, in part because they are brilliant and beautiful, and in part to honor the fish by dressing him in his best. When completed, the model needed a large space to be properly displayed. Addrien Marx, owner of Rovero's service station in Seeley Lake, offered a spot on a wall above the cash registers where everyone could see it.

Marx told me that customers often inquire about the fish, and those who heard about the background liked to tell it to others. So that's the story of how I messed up one big fish, but also how a community gave the giant cutthroat of Seeley Lake a second life.

HOME WATERS

I DO NOT FISH ALONE on the Blackfoot River, ever, even though now I mostly fish it by myself. When I'm on the water, and especially when no one else is around, I feel the presence of the generations of my family whose stories run through it. Thanks to geology and hard rock the river hasn't changed much from the time the Reverend Maclean brought his sons here, when he brought young George Croonenberghs along to carry his basket, when his son Paul swam laughing down the river with his rod held high. The Burns family was added along the way, and when I was old enough to join the men on the river, we'd go out together, maybe five or six rods all told, and we'd split up the river.

Ken Burns was everybody's favorite uncle, my mother's beloved brother, and a man who knew how to have a good time. He'd stayed in Wolf Creek and never grown rich, but he said if he could change anything in his life, he'd have ham for breakfast every morning and mayonnaise on both sides of his sandwich for lunch. I'd often join up with him and trade casts into the same deep hole—sometimes even to the same spot to the same fish—and we enjoyed the comradeship.

Ken's wife, Dottie, was the only woman family member I know of who fished. In the spring when Little Prickly Pear Creek was running muddy and high, she would get one of Ken's Prince Albert tobacco cans and fill it with dirt and worms. Then she'd take a rod and go down to a nice hole on the Little Prickly Pear right behind the chicken coops, hook up a gob of worms, and sling the outfit into the hole. When a fish gobbled the worms she'd turn around, put the rod on her shoulder, and run like hell up the bank, dragging the fish out of the water. Like Ken, she made a good life out of very little in the material way: for years her Christmas presents to my sister and me were pajamas she had sewn out of old chicken feed sacks; they were scratchy, but we—or at least I—couldn't get enough of them. My favorite present from her, though, was a Sons of the Pioneers record album with songs like "Cool Water" and "Tumbling Tumbleweeds." "It's about us," my aunt told me. "We are the sons and daughters of the pioneers."

Memory can and should be more than a bridge to the past. It's also a way to see yourself as a thread in a broad fabric long in the making. By the time my own sons, Danny and JohnFitz, were able to fish the Blackfoot River with me, the older generation had been whittled down in number. Nowhere was the spirit we all shared more present, though, than at the Muchmore Hole—with its river-wide reef and its massive whirlpool covered with foam, and links to the past. It had taken me a lifetime to reach this place and to connect with the enormous rainbow trout that had risen in a curving arc, a dream fish that now threatened to spit the fly back in my face.

My fishing partner Jay swiped the net time and time again until finally the fish tired enough to be held half in and half out of the net. Jay gingerly carried both fish and net to shore. We took only a couple of hurried photographs, because the fish was exhausted and needed to be back in the water as quickly as possible. When I placed him in the river, he turned belly up. Fish die that way. I righted him and turned his head upstream into the oxygen-rich water. He finned to stay in place, his gills panting. A minute passed, maybe more. Finally, he turned and slowly began to move back into the current toward the deep water, and then with a single rippling thrust of his entire body he shot into the depths and disappeared.

I walked over to a big snag lying on the bank up near the high-water mark. The river had stripped off the bark and polished the tree trunk to a bone-white smoothness. A forked branch stuck up from the snag, and I sat on the trunk and leaned back into the branch. I was comfortable there. Strobe-like images of a fish's glaring eye, an iridescent strip of scarlet, and a salmon-sized head flashed in my mind's eye. I'd never seen a Blackfoot rainbow that big before, never. The present moment slowly came back into focus: a turquoise sky wind-stripped of clouds, bright sparkling sunshine, and the endlessly moving river.

Life doesn't stop when you reach a peak; it moves on as before, just as a river does after a fight with a big fish. On a day like this, though, and after a rainbow trout like that one, the river merged the life of the spirit with the act of fly fishing, a legacy endlessly renewed by the passage of waters. Home waters.

NOTES AND ACKNOWLEDGMENTS

Home Waters is a family affair, but many people contributed to it. The project began when my friend Jay Proops asked me to write a short account for his group, the Anglers Club of Chicago, about hooking a big rainbow trout in the Muchmore Hole on the Blackfoot River, which his ranch borders. From there, it became a longer story in *Big Sky Journal*, thanks to the support of Seeley Lake friend Jenny Rohrer. Peter Hubbard, executive editor at William Morrow, read that story and asked if I was interested in enlarging the scope and making it a book. Proops and others read drafts or parts of *Home Waters*, and their criticisms, corrections, and encouragement helped make it fuller and more accurate: thanks go to Jason Borger, Alec Underwood, Cheryl Hughes, Kelly Andersson, Rick Kogan, and my longtime agent and friend Jennifer Lyons. Ron Cox read the section on the Lewis journey through the Blackfoot Valley, which I would not have attempted without his help and direction; Jim Hepworth read the section on the dates of Paul Maclean's life, which he had helped to establish.

James R. Habeck, emeritus professor of ecology at the University of Montana, has been the spark, the central clearinghouse, and a leading contributor to an ongoing effort by a group of researchers, myself included, who have spent years gathering biographical material about the Maclean and Burns families. The group has dug up and shared newspaper, archival, and other records going back more than a century. Others who have worked on this project include the aforementioned Jim Hepworth, a retired professor of English at Lewis-Clark State College in Lewiston, Idaho; Rebecca McCarthy, a former student of my father's; and my sister, Jean Maclean Snyder. Another contributor, Kim Briggeman of the *Missoulian*, has also written about the family and Montana's fishing history in numerous authoritative articles for his newspaper. This group has gathered more information than any single person, even a family member, could have accomplished alone.

The references to fishing and fishing equipment on the Lewis and Clark expedition are based on the expedition journals and "Undaunted Anglers," an essay about the expedition's fishing gear and exploits by Marshall E. Bloom, M.D., who lives and fishes in the Bitterroot Valley. Bloom is associate director for science management at the Rocky Mountain Laboratories in Hamilton, Montana, a division of the National Institutes of Health, and chief of the Biology of Vector-Borne Viruses section. Robert N. Bergantino, of the Montana Bureau of Mines and Geology, shared his maps and data about the locations of the Lewis campsites, and graciously corrected my misapprehensions. Gary E. Moulton, editor of the authoritative University of Nebraska edition of the Lewis and Clark Journals, cites Bergantino's data as the benchmark for locating the expedition's campsites. I used the Moulton edition for all references to the journals.

The section on the effects of the movie *A River Runs Through It* on the Blackfoot River is based on "Blackfoot Restoration as a National Model," a talk given by David Brooks, executive director for Montana Trout Unlimited, at the In the Footsteps of Norman Maclean Festival in Missoula, Montana, in September 2017, which I attended. He later shared his notes with me and read over the section on the history of the Blackfoot River fishery, providing valuable comments and edits.

At that year's festival, Stephenie Ambrose Tubbs presented a paper, "What's in a Name? Meriwether Lewis and the Blackfoot River Valley," in which she argued for changing the name of Monture Creek back to Seaman's Creek, in

honor of Meriwether Lewis's dog Seaman, for whom it originally was named. "Seaman deserves his creek!" she told
me. Local residents cite problems with property and water
rights and other issues, however, and the name has remained
Monture Creek, for an early fur trapper and trader. Ms. Tubbs,
the daughter of Stephen Ambrose, author of *Undaunted Courage: Meriwether Lewis, Thomas Jefferson, and the Opening of
the American West,* is coauthor with Clay Straus Jenkinson of
*The Lewis and Clark Companion: An Encyclopedic Guide to
the Voyage of Discovery.* Her family for a time had a summer
cabin on the North Fork of the Blackfoot River.

The account of Gifford Pinchot's trip through Swan and
Clearwater country, an unpublished manuscript, titled "Trip
GP and Jack Monroe Up Swan River, June 1896," is among
a massive Pinchot collection at the Library of Congress that
contains two million items in over three thousand contain-
ers taking up twelve hundred twenty linear feet. A copy of
the handwritten daily diary from that trip came to me from
Cheryl Hughes, a longtime educational consultant based
in Missoula, who found it among his papers at the Pinchot
ancestral home, Grey Towers in Milford, Pennsylvania, now
a National Historic Site.

Alec Underwood, federal conservation campaigns director at the Montana Wildlife Federation, made his extensive
photo collection of fishing and the Blackfoot River available

for the book. His advice and general assistance with illustrations has also been invaluable. Alec hails from upstate New York, but after reading *A River Runs through It* as a youth he determined to move to Montana. I once invited him for an evening's fishing on a favorite stretch of the Blackfoot. The spot I'd picked turned out to be the first place Alec had fished the river after coming out to Montana, and for him the trip was a reminder of his own Blackfoot River legacy.

Marvin Tupper Jones, a professional photographer and friend, was generous with his time and skills in making useful images from old snapshots, postcards, and photos.

The Montana Historical Society in Helena was helpful in gathering images, especially postcard views from early in the twentieth century.

My sister, Jean, was helpful with photographs: special thanks to her husband, Joel Snyder, for his print of Norman's photo of Paul Maclean fishing.

The section on the City News Bureau of Chicago was read by one of my oldest and best friends, Bernie Judge. He and I started at City News the same year, 1964. We scored our first verbatim appearance in a Chicago daily on a police blotter story he'd been alerted to by a cop friend of his. I wrote it up and the *Chicago American* newspaper published it word for word as written, a rare coup for City News, which functioned mostly as a tip sheet for the dailies. We were each awarded a $5-a-week raise, almost a 10 percent increase. Bernie, who had never taken a journalism course and lacked a college degree, went on to a brilliantly successful career in Chicago journalism. He joined the *Tribune* after I did, at my urging, and he and I worked on several stories with shared bylines. He became the *Tribune*'s city editor and supervised two projects that won Pulitzer Prizes. Along the way he stood up for me as best man when Frances and I were married in 1968 by Judge Julius J. Hoffman, known as Julius the Just for his tough sentences of mob figures, before his downfall in the Chicago Seven trial. Bernie left the *Tribune* to return to the City News Bureau as editor and general manager. He left there to become metropolitan editor of the *Sun-Times*, just as he had been at the *Tribune*, an extraordinary feat in the hotly competitive world of Chicago journalism of that day. He finished his career as editor and vice president of the *Chicago Daily Law Bulletin*. There, he ran freelance stories by my son, John Fitzroy, who became a lawyer after he left City News, where Bernie had hired him.

When Bernie was diagnosed with inoperable cancer in 2019, he announced the news quietly, in an email distributed to friends. He refused treatment and died that June surrounded by his large and loving family, full of courage to the end. On his deathbed, his son BJ told me, he slashed his hand across his throat in the universal gesture of finality when he'd had enough. I asked his widow Kimbeth if she and the family were okay with me writing about that scene. "It's strong stuff all right," she wrote back. "But that's who he was, we all agreed." Mourners by the hundreds filled the pews of St. Giles Catholic Church in Oak Park for his funeral Mass.

INDEX

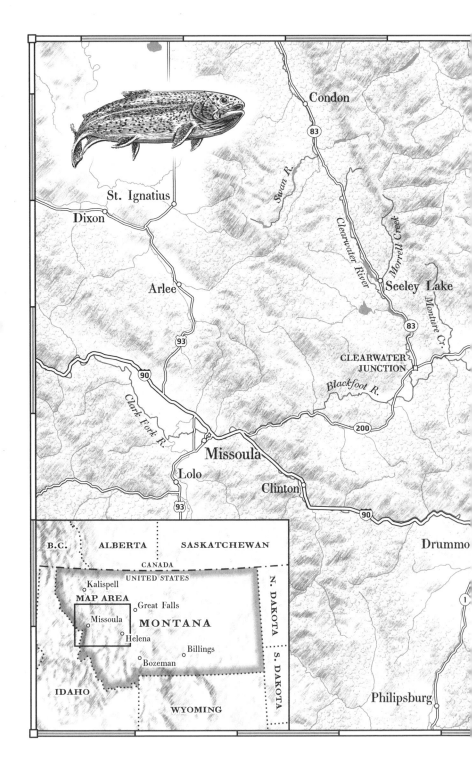

Condon

83

Swan R.

Clearwater River

Morrell Creek

St. Ignatius

Dixon

Seeley Lake

83

Moniture Cr.

Arlee

93

CLEARWATER
JUNCTION

90

Clark Fork R.

Blackfoot R.

200

Missoula

Lolo

Clinton

90

Drummo

93

1

B.C. | ALBERTA | SASKATCHEWAN

CANADA

UNITED STATES

N. DAKOTA

Kalispell

MAP AREA

Great Falls

Missoula

MONTANA

Helena

S. DAKOTA

Billings

Bozeman

IDAHO

WYOMING

Philipsburg